Tarantulas in the Vivarium

Tarantulas in the Vivarium

Habits, husbandry, and breeding

by Peter Klaas

Technical editing of the English Translation
by Paul Gritis

Krieger Publishing Company
Malabar, Florida
2001

Front cover photo: *Brachypelma mesomelas*

Original German Edition, *Vogelspinnen im Terrarium,* 1989
English Edition 2001 with updated taxonomy
Translation by John Hackworth
Technical Editing by Paul Gritis

Printed and Published by
KRIEGER PUBLISHING COMPANY
KRIEGER DRIVE
MALABAR, FLORIDA 32950

FROM A DECLARATION OF PRINCIPLES JOINTLY ADOPTED BY
A COMMITTEE OF THE AMERICAN BAR ASSOCIATION AND A
COMMITTEE OF PUBLISHERS:
This publication is designed to provide accurate and authoritative information in regard to the
subject matter covered. It is sold with the understanding that the publisher is not engaged in
rendering legal, accounting, or other professional service. If legal advice or other expert
assistance is required, the services of a competent profesional person should be sought.

Library of Congress Cataloging-in-Publication Data

Klaas, Peter.
     [Vogelspinnen Im Terrarium. English]
     Tarantulas in the vivarium : habits, husbandry, and breeding / Peter Klaas ;
[original translation by John Hackworth].
          p.   cm.
     Includes bibliographical references and index.
     ISBN 1-57524-018-1 (hardcover : alk. paper)
     1. Tarantulas as pets.   2. Tarantulas.   3. Vivariums.   I. Title.

SF459.T37 K6313 2000
639′.7—dc21   99-087619

10 9 8 7 6 5 4 3 2

Editor's Preface to the English Translation

Tarantulas and other spiders, as well as other animals like snakes, have been regarded by most of humanity for centuries with fear and loathing, but by a few observers with fascination and scientific interest.

Like snakes, tarantulas have in recent years undergone a renaissance, in that increasing numbers of people have become interested in maintaining and breeding them in captivity. Only a few years ago arachnids were scarcely to be seen even in large zoos. Today large numbers of them, of a wide variety of species, are encountered in the pet trade, zoos and other institutions.

The amount of published information on identification, natural history, care and captive breeding of tarantulas has greatly increased in recent years. Much of the older literature aimed at the arachnid hobbyist, as little as there has been, is inadequate. Much of the hobbyist literature has been written by persons without first-hand experience, or at any rate, without extensive experience with several species. Bad advice and speculation have been presented as fact, to the detriment of the spiders and the hobby.

The book before you now is a contribution by a German hobbyist based upon his practical experience keeping, breeding, and raising numerous species. It is to the best of my knowledge the first English translation of a German guide to tarantulas.

It is hoped that this English translation will make available to English-speaking readers the wide experience of the author and his colleagues. Perhaps it will help to initiate contact between North American and European hobbyists. It is also hoped that this book will contribute toward eliminating fear and misunderstanding between humans and tarantulas (which is, of course, strictly one-sided).

Scientific Names, Common Names and Terminology

Determining the correct scientific name to be used for a given tarantula is often a difficult process. The few qualified experts may disagree as to the valid name. For the average tarantula keeper, gaining access to the literature of recent taxonomic changes may be difficult, and understanding it even more so. Added to this, the accurate identification of tarantulas, especially those without good locality information, is often very difficult. In most cases it cannot be done accurately without detailed examination of the spider (sometimes under a microscope).

The scientific names used here are those used by the author, who provided a listing of name changes occurring after the publication (1989) of the original German edition. Incorporating these changes resulted in the species accounts no longer remaining in alphabetical order. Invalid names are listed as they occur alphabetically with the new names listed on the next line. New names have been inserted into the correct alphabetical order as well but are cross-referenced to the invalid name for the species account. Thus, the original order of the German text is maintained. In one instance, namely *Dugesiella anax,* the more widely used generic name *Aphonopelma* is placed in brackets [ ]. This was done because this American spider is more commonly known in the English-speaking world under that generic name.

Common names used in the English translation are in most cases those established by the American Arachnological Society (Breene, 1997). These are not translations of the German common names, and so are not the work of Peter Klaas but are my responsibility and I assume all criticism.

Anatomical and other biological terminology reflects European usage, which differs in some regards from American. In case of confusion, reference to the standard work by Foelix (1996) may help American readers.

I recommend that readers of this book join the American Tarantula Society (contact American Tarantula Society, P.O. Box 756, Carlsbad NM 88221; telephone 505-885-8406.
email: neatspider@aol.com
website: atshq.org

References Cited

Breene, R. G. (Chairman) 1997. *Common Names of Arachnids*. 2nd Edition. (American Tarantula Society/American Arachnological Society Committee on Common Names of Arachnids) 74 pp.

Foelix, R. 1996. *Biology of Spiders*. 2nd Edition. (Oxford University Press) 330 pp.

Paul Gritis
1999

Dedication and Acknowledgments

This book is dedicated to my parents, brothers and sisters whose patience, tolerance and understanding have allowed my hobby of tarantulas to increase to its present extent. Patience because telephone conservations with other enthusiasts, sometimes lasting several hours, occasionally disturbed the peace in our household, and tolerance of escaped food insects which frequently wandered freely around the home.

I must also not miss the opportunity to thank the many people who assisted in so many ways in the creation of this volume. I was provided with many species of tarantulas by Kurt Nicolaisen of Denmark, Dieter Scholz and Frauke Selter (Bonn) whose hospitality I shall never forget and who assisted me to take some excellent photographs.

The drawings prepared by the designer Klaus Richter of Düsseldorf are perfect in every detail. For the critical review of the manuscript, I must express my thanks to Dr. H. Schröder of the Senckenberg Museum in Frankfurt am Main and Rainer Stawikowski of Verlag Eugen Ulmer. My long-term friendship with Mathias Forst, the head of the Insectarium of Cologne Zoological Gardens produced many interesting discussions and was one of the main reasons for the manuscript being produced. I was extremely honored that Prof. Dr. Günther Nogge, the Director of Cologne Zoological Gardens, elected to write a foreword to this volume.

Peter Klaas
Cologne, May 1989

Foreword

There is hardly any group of animals which causes so much human antipathy as spiders. On the other hand, the number of spider enthusiasts and keepers of tarantulas increases each year. In the 1970s Horst Stern produced two superlative television films and together with Ernst Kullmann published a book entitled *Leben am seidenen Faden (Life on Silken Threads)* which introduced spiders to several million viewers. Quoting a scientist from the 1950s Stern remarked that "even today we are regularly bombarded with newspaper reports about giant spiders lurking in cellars to spring silently from the ceiling to attack unsuspecting humans, biting them on the back of the neck to sever their nerves and suck away their life blood. They have already claimed several dozen victims."

The present volume, written by an amateur who is nevertheless an expert, is a further contribution which will serve to remove some of the prejudice still widely held against spiders. Peter Klaas, an acknowledged expert in this field of captive husbandry, has presented, in both words and pictures, tarantulas, their systematic position, anatomy and habits. He makes suggestions about the correct construction and furnishing of vivaria, the feeding and breeding of tarantulas as well as the legal and safety requirements which must be observed when keeping these animals. Over 30 species are individually discussed giving details about their husbandry and breeding as well as any specific peculiarities or requirements.

There is, however, a further reason why tarantulas deserve to be more popular among animal lovers. The German federal laws which came into force on 1 January 1987 do not only extend strict protection to all species covered by the Washington (CITES) Agreement. They also include European amphibians, reptiles, birds as well as all native mammals and various other groups of animals although these species may already have been bred in captivity for generations. The prohibition of marketing animals of protected species is an attempt to reduce the numbers of wild animals kept in captivity and thus a measure—although obviously an insufficient measure—to protect nature and wild populations.

Many animal lovers, keepers and breeders are so subjected to mountains of bureaucratic forms, licenses, advertising regulations and standards as well as ever increasing official charges that they are compelled to give up their hobby. Others, however, with a deep rooted love of animals, change to such species which are not yet subjected to such strict regulations. For anyone with an interest in keeping tarantulas in captivity, the present book will be a guide for the husbandry and breeding of those animals.

Prof. Dr. Günther Nogge

Contents

Frequently Kept Tarantula Species

Contents

The Natural History and Distribution of Tarantulas

Evolutionary History

The first tarantulas lived around 250–300 million years ago during the Carboniferous. Fossil finds from that period have shown that many antenna-less forms (Chelicerata) were very similar to the present day species. During the Carboniferous there were horseshoe crabs (of the order Xiphosura) with lengths of around 60 cm. Nowadays these extremely interesting crabs are restricted to a few species on the coasts of North America and southern Asia.

Fossil finds of whiptailed scorpions and other spider-like forms which lived around 350 million years ago allow us to trace — even if only very loosely — the evolution of the present day Chelicerate fauna.

In the Tertiary period, around 30 million years ago, tarantulas were part of the fauna of Europe. Today there are only a few true tarantulas of the subfamily Ischnocolinae to be found in Europe. Three of these species live in southern Spain. It is interesting to note that the morphology of tarantulas since their origin has essentially remained the same while during the same period entire Orders of other animals became extinct.

The capability of tarantulas to survive in constantly changing environments is one of the reasons why this early form of arachnid fauna still exists today.

Relationships

The relatives of the tarantulas, those belonging to the order Araneae (spiders), include no less than around 34,000 species of spiders. For terrarium keepers, there are a number of other arachnids apart from tarantulas which are of interest. Examples of these are the giant orbweaver spiders of the genus *Nephila,* the webs of which may be 1.5 m in diameter and are in every decent zoological collection. Furthermore, every arachnid enthusiast, when given the opportunity, will not fail to return from a Mediterranean vacation without some of the large spiders of the family Lycosidae so that their extremely interesting method of brood protection may be closely observed in the vivarium.

And who does not know the black widow, *Latrodectus mactans,* that spherical spider of the family Theridiidae, the venom of which can also be fatal for humans?

Other, more distant relatives of tarantulas of various orders have also proved to be interesting captives. Examples of this are scorpions, which, with around 600 species inhabit all warmer parts of the earth. These have become interesting captives and are much in demand and regularly imported. More rarely there are arachnid enthusiasts who keep whipscorpions and windscorpions.

Fig. 1. (above) *Lycosa tarentula,* the Italian tarantula is a harmless wolf spider.
Fig. 2. (below left) A beautifully colored wolf spider (Lycosidae) from Panama.

Fig. 3. (below right) Order: Opiliones. In tropical regions some of the relatives of spiders are quite bizarre in appearance.

Fig. 4. (above left) *Latrodectus mactans*: the southern black widow.
Fig. 5. (below left) Suborder: Mesothelae. The very rare segmented spiders of the genus *Liphistius* have primitive developmental stages.
Fig. 6. (above right) Order: Amblypygi. The tailless whipscorpions live in the tropics. Some specimens may have legs up to 20 cm long. The animal in the photograph is *Admetus pumilio* with nymphs.
Fig. 7. (center right) *Admetus pumilio* molting.
Fig. 8. (below right) *Scolopendra cingulata*, a centipede.

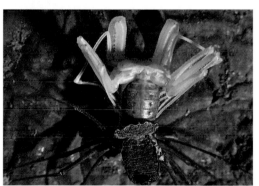

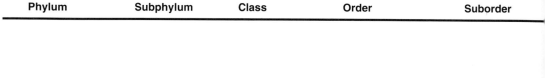

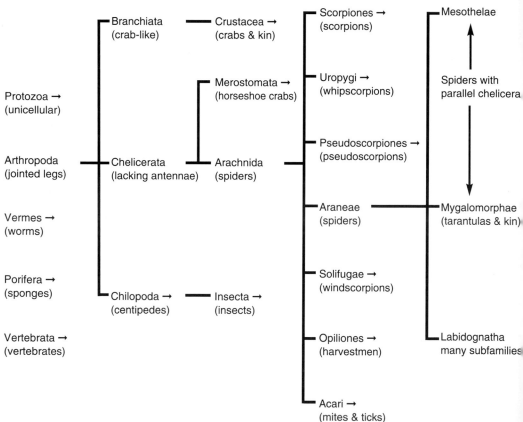

Evolutionary tree and
systematic arrangement of tarantulas
(Theraphosidae)

Family	Subfamily	Group	Genera (examples)

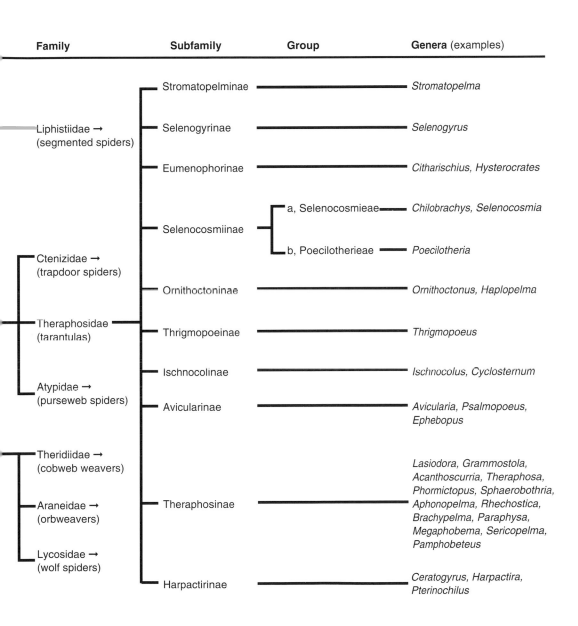

Fig. 9. *Heteropoda venatoria.* A giant huntsman spider from Sri Lanka.

Evolutionary Tree

With only a little practice it is not too difficult for an enthusiast to classify animals systematically. Using as an example one of the most popular tarantulas, the Mexican redknee tarantula *Brachypelma smithi*, we should all try at least once to be "systematists." The branches which are most important for our purposes can be clearly seen from the evolutionary tree found on pages 4–5. Naturally the other groups of animals mentioned are also further subdivided to avoid any confusion in this connection.

The Mexican redleg tarantula is one of many species of the genus *Brachypelma*. If one follows the evolutionary tree further back, it can be seen that the genus *Brachypelma* and some other genera belong to the subfamily Grammostolinae. A family may be composed of many subfamilies. In this

case, the Grammostolinae belong to the family Theraphosidae. Together with the trapdoor spiders and the purseweb spiders, these families belong to the suborder of Mygalomorphae.

By further grouping this suborder one arrives at the order of spiders (Araneae) and if one continues on this path one will finally receive a sort of "calling card" of the given species of spider:

Phylum: Arthropoda (Jointed feet)
Subphylum: Chelicerata (Lacking antennae)
Class: Arachnida (Spiders and kin)
Order: Araneae (Spiders)
Suborder: Mygalomorphae (Tarantula-like)
Family: Theraphosidae (Tarantulas)
Subfamily: Grammostolinae
Genus: *Brachypelma*
Species: *smithi*

If one arranges tarantulas in this way it will soon be discovered that working with such a "dry" subject as systematics can also be rewarding.

The External Anatomy of a Tarantula

The external appearance of a tarantula is best explained by using line drawings. It is unavoidable to use scientific terminology.

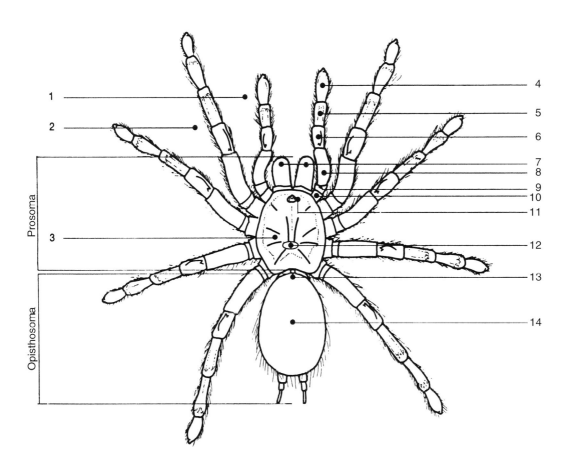

External Anatomy of a Tarantula (from above)

1. Pedipalp
2. Walking legs
3. Cephalothorax
4. Tarsus
5. Tibia
6. Patella
7. Chelicera
8. Femur
9. Trochanter
10. Coxa (with pedipalp plate)
11. Eye ridge
12. Thorax groove
13. Pedicel
14. Abdomen

Many enthusiasts are a little wary of scientific terminology but with a little practice it soon becomes familiar. It would be totally impossible to describe the various parts of a tarantula without using the correct scientific terms.

Cephalothorax

As well as the extremities, the front part of the body of spiders (the cephalothorax or prosoma) consists, on the upper side, of a head and thorax (carapace) and on the underside of a star-shaped plate (sternum). The sternum is moveably attached to the labium. Together with the maxillae attached to the coxa on both the left and the right, the labium allows the spiders to eat. Whereas in insects the head and thorax are always separate, those of the spider are always fused.

The carapace serves several purposes. Its first is to support the spider's body and its second is that it provides a place for the attachment of other bodily parts. The head section of the carapace has a so-called eye ridge (or eye pod) upon the surface of which eight minute eyes are symmetrically arranged.

On the rear one-third of the carapace, the thoracic furrow can be found. From the center of this, the radial furrows (striae radiantes) run to the bases of the legs. Inside the spider, the thoracic furrow and the radial furrows provide attachment points for the leg musculature and the sucking stomach muscles. The first pair of radial furrows are usually easily recognizable and delimit the head part of the carapace from the thoracic part.

In the case of *Brachypelma emilia* (Mexican redleg tarantula) this is particularly easy to see because the head section is a totally different color than the thoracic section.

Extremities

The first pair of extremities of a spider are the chelicerae. They are best seen from below the carapace. In the case of tarantulas the fangs lie parallel to the longitudinal axis of the body and move upwards and downwards (not sideways). Because of these characteristics, tarantulas are assigned to the Suborder Orthognatha spiders which also include the trapdoor spiders, purseweb spiders and others. When at rest, the fangs lie in a groove in the chelicerae.

The chelicerae contain the elongated venom glands, and the fangs inject the venom into the victim. The venom channel opens at the tip of the fangs. The mandibular "feelers" (pedipalps) are attached next to the chelicerae. In young and females, these organs, which actually belong to the mouth mechanism, are converted into locomotion and sensory legs.

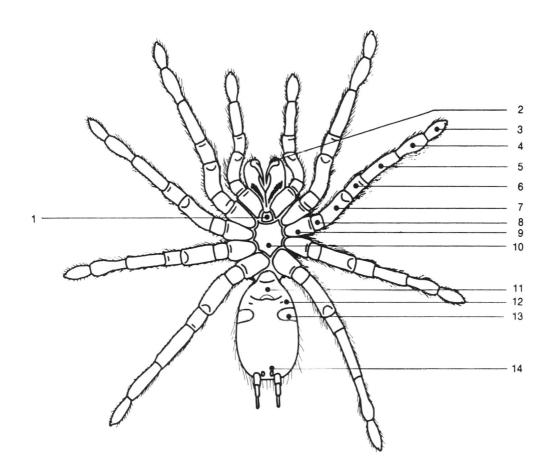

External Anatomy of a Tarantula (from below)

1. Labium
2. Fangs
3. Tarsus
4. Metatarsus
5. Tibia
6. Patella
7. Femur
8. Trochanter
9. Coxa
10. Sternum
11. Seminal receptacle
12. Stigma
13. Opening to book lung
14. Spinnerets

Fig. 10. The chelicerae are arranged in pairs. In some species, the fangs may be up to 17 mm long.

Fig. 11. (above) The first leg of a male *Phormictopus cancerides* with tibial spurs. (below) The pedipalp of *P. cancerides* with bulbs.

The individual segments of the pedipalps are named in the line drawing of the dorsal view of a tarantula. After the final molt (maturity molt) the pedipalps of males appear totally different. At the ends of the pedipalps, mature males have the so-called bulbs (cymbium). These are the primary sexual organs, which usually are pear-shaped storage containers that come to a fine point. In these bulbs, sperm for the later fertilization of females is stored. The shape of the bulbs can be used to identify individual species. For arachnid hobbyists, however, the identification of tarantulas by means of the bulbs is almost impossible because simply not enough males are available and such identification is only possible on dead animals.

The sections of the following four pairs of legs are designated as coxa, trochanter, femur, patella, tibia, metatarsus and tarsus. On the end of the tarsus are usually two retractile claws which are withdrawn into two small "hair pads" or scopulae. In tarantulas of the genus *Avicularia* these often brightly colored pads are particularly easy to see when the animal is moving. In mature males, the limbs can be additionally modified. In this case, the tibia of the first pair of legs often has one or two tibial spurs. These are small projecting hooks which help to position the female during mating.

The pedipalp bulbs and tibial spurs are secondary sexual characteristics which allow quick and easy distinction between males and females.

Abdomen

The abdomen is attached to the cephalothorax by a short, almost indiscernible connecting piece (pedicel). Actually, the name abdomen is incorrect because it comes from the nomenclature of the insect world and cannot directly be applied to spiders. However, in arachnology it has become so ingrained that nowadays rarely anyone objects to it.

The abdomen—one of the most sensitive parts of the body of a spider—takes over many bodily functions. As a storage for food and energy it enables the spider to fast for many months. All important organs are contained in the abdomen, for example the tube-like heart, the blood circulation, parts of the digestive tract, the ovaries, sexual organs, silk glands etc. However, here we do not wish to occupy ourselves with the complicated internal anatomy of a spider, but rather with its easily identifiable external body parts.

At the rear of the body two long and easily identifiable spinnerets and also two smaller spinnerets are capable of moving independently of one another. On the underside of the abdomen the two openings of the entrances to the book lungs can be seen.

Within these are the internal concealed book lungs. The stigma of the first book lungs end in the so-called epigastric furrow into which sexual organs of the animals also open. The two stigmata of the rear lungs end near the epigastric furrow.

Tactile and Sensory Hairs

The unique hairs of tarantulas are one of the most amazing wonders of nature. Frequently the individual hairs are so small that they cannot be seen with the naked eye and are only visible through an electron microscope.

Sensory and Olfactory Hairs. The olfactory hairs which are mainly on the pedipalps and first pair of legs are indeed the most interesting phenomenon in the world of arthropods. Within a fraction of a second, the chemotactile receptors of these hairs can pass relevant information to the spider's brain. It is in this way that prey is recognized! It has not yet been determined if spiders use pheromones (sexual odors) to locate sexual partners as is common in the insect world. Nevertheless, for several reasons it is believed that pheromones exist in spiders. For instance, it is easy to incite a male tarantula to exhibit courtship behavior by using forceps to hold a small piece of the female's web in front of his pedipalps.

Tactile Hairs. The entire body of a spider, especially the legs, is covered with an even layer of tactile hairs which serves a variety of functions. Next to the olfactory hairs these are the most important of a spider's sensory hairs. Using the tactile hairs, the tarantula is able to locate its prey. The tactile hairs are so sensitive that their owner is not only able to determine the distance of its prey, but also its direction and size. Each tactile hair detects all mechanical waves such as shocks and vibrations. Along with the special sensory organs, the tactile hairs are the most important mechanoreceptors.

Adhesive Hairs. The tarsus and metatarsus of many tarantulas are frequently covered in a thick pad of fine adhesive hairs (clinging pads or scopula). For a considerable time nothing was known about the function of these hairs. However in the meantime, researchers now appear to agree: the solution to the problem is simply adhesion. The minute adhesive hairs, which are branched at the end, make full use of the fine layer of water on the surface of every object. As a result of the capillary action between the layer of water and the end of the clinging hairs, the scopula are able to take a firm hold on whatever is beneath them. When placed on a pane of glass which had been specially treated to ensure that it was completely dry, the spider slid off. These pads

of hair are often brightly colored, the result of light refraction, as in the case of the beautiful butterflies of the tropics.

Other Hairs. Many New World tarantulas also have the so-called stinging hairs on their abdomen. These are very loosely attached to the abdominal skin. By rubbing their hind legs together, the spiders can loosen these hairs from their anchor points and throw them into the air. Coming into contact with these minute hairs causes itching and skin inflammation which may last for several days. Should they come into contact with the mucous membranes or the respiratory tract they may cause severe coughing bouts. Spiders which have such a defense mechanism are commonly called urticating spiders. Using the so-called "audio" hairs, tarantulas can also detect some low frequency sound waves.

Fig. 13. *Pandinus imperator* is one of the largest scorpions of West Africa. Shown is a female with young.

Other Orders of Arachnids Important for the Vivarium

On the following pages, we shall briefly consider the other orders of arachnids which are sometimes kept in vivaria. We shall not only consider animals which are suitable for keeping in vivaria, but also those which can be raised as food and those which may be dangerous to our vivarium animals.

Order: Scorpiones (Scorpions)

Next to spiders, these are the most frequently kept Chelicerata. The ends of the chelicerae always end in a pincer-like organ with which they hold their prey or sexual partner. The rear part of the body is clearly divided into seven sections. The tail-like postabdomen has five sections ending in a sharp, venomous spine. All give birth to live young.
Euscorpius italicus
(Italian scorpion)
Pandinus imperator
(African giant scorpion)

Order: Uropygi (Whipscorpions)

They are often kept in vivaria, and have very secretive lifestyles. The mandibular

feelers are modified to form claws. The first pair of legs are extremely thin and antenna-like. The postabdomen is thin and segmented, and some species spray acetic acid.

Order: Solifugae (Windscorpions)

These are very desirable vivarium subjects but are difficult to keep. The body is like that of a spider. The abdomen is divided into ten segments. Chelicerae are without venom glands, but are modified into powerful gripping organs. They are nocturnal desert dwellers, and extremely fast runners that catch insects expertly.

Fig. 14. Order: Uropygi, a whipscorpion.

Order: Pseudoscorpiones (Pseudoscorpions)

Frequently found on the forest floor, these scorpion-like species may grow to 7 mm. Abdomens are divided into segments. There is no postabdomen or venom spine, and they are occasionally kept in the terrarium. Book scorpions of the genus *Chelifer* are well known.

Order: Acari (Mites)

This is the largest order with around 40,000 species. In the vivarium this order is very important as the following:

– predators on food insects
– parasites on vivarium animals
– species which live symbiotically, e.g., between the chelicerae of spiders

Fig. 15. (above) Order: Solifugae. Windscorpions are extremely fast hunters. Their fangs can easily pierce human skin and they can inflict a painful bite. The solifuges do not have venom glands.
Fig. 16. (below) Mites attached along the side of a scorpion (*Opistophthalmus*).

– parasites on plants
– species living in house dust causing all types of allergies.

Where Do Tarantulas Live?

According to their preferred habitat, tarantulas may be divided into three groups:

– arboreal species
– terrestrial species
– subterranean species

However, all three may live very close to one another in the same biotope.
Many tarantula species of the subfamily Avicularinae are arboreal. These are typical climbing spiders which because of the shape of their bodies and their build, are particularly suited to life in bushes and trees. In general, these animals usually have a relatively small abdomen and the tarsi and metatarsi have large adhesive pads. Equipped in this way, these animals are able to climb on clean panes of glass without any great effort.

It is worth mentioning that when threatened, some species such as *Avicularia metallica* can jump short distances and may free-fall away from danger. To do this they spread their hairy legs to form a sort of parachute and float to the ground. Perhaps this is one reason why a common name for these animals is bird spiders!

Figs. 17 and 18. (above and below) *Avicularia metallica* in a swampy area of Ecuador.

Because some species occur over large areas, they may inhabit very divergent biotopes. Figs. 17 and 18 show a normally

arboreal species, *Avicularia metallica*, which was photographed in a swampy area of the eastern Andes in Ecuador. There it lived on the large leaves of *Parnassia* plants. In French Guiana, *Avicularia* can even be found in the chimneys of old houses and sometimes is quite common. In the floodlands of the Amazon which are often under 3 or 4 meters of water for months, *A. metallica* has adapted to a life among the forest trees. It is either beneath the bark of trees or among the branches and leaves, where it spins a large web in which it lives.

Fig. 19 shows a *Psalmopoeus* species which was photographed among the roots of a fallen tree on the banks of a river in the tropical rain forest of central Panama. The *Paraphysa pulcherrimaklaasi* shown in Fig. 76 was found in the reservoir of a bromeliad plant in the rain forest of Ecuador. Many Asian tarantulas, especially of the genus *Poecilotheria*, inhabit trees, bushes and even houses. The most interesting tarantulas for hobbyists are probably the purely terrestrial species. The genus *Brachypelma*, in particular, offers a large number of some of the most beautiful and easily kept tarantulas.

All terrestrial spiders have a very compact appearance, although their hind quarters may assume imposing dimensions. Females carrying eggs may have an abdomen as large as a chicken's egg. The extremities are relatively short and stout and thus not

Fig. 19. A specimen of *Psalmopoeus* among the roots of a fallen tree in the tropical rain forest in Panama.

Fig. 20. (above) Biotope of *Poecilotheria fasciata*. As well as *P. fasciata* we also found frogs and lizards (*Kaloula ceylanica, Varanus salvator,* some wonderful *Cyrtodactylus* species) and some colorful kingfishers.

Fig. 21. (below left) Habitat of *Poecilotheria fasciata* in Sri Lanka. This species lives in hollow trees and in knotholes. Because of its very secretive lifestyle and great rarity, this is one of the most expensive tarantulas in the world.

Fig. 22. (below right) Before catching the animal, the appearance of the tree had to be altered somewhat.

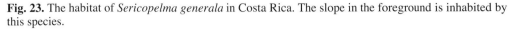

Fig. 23. The habitat of *Sericopelma generala* in Costa Rica. The slope in the foreground is inhabited by this species.

particularly suitable for climbing.

The group of subterranean tarantulas contains some highly interesting species. If one disregards the families Atypidae and Ctenizidae which spend some of their time in tunnels that they excavate themselves, among the family Theraphosidae a large number of species lead a sedentary, secretive underground life. Some species dig deep, nearly vertical tunnels at the entrances to which they sit at night waiting for prey to pass by. Typical examples of such species are the frequently imported "Thai tarantulas" of the subfamilies Selenocosmiinae and Ornithoctoninae. The almost unbelievable number of species is one of the reasons why there is great confusion as to which genera and species individuals belong.

The Kenyan species *Citharischius crawshayi* lives in tunnels several meters deep in the hard laterite soil and only rarely comes to the surface. *Theraphosa blondi* from the rain forests of Venezuela lives deep among the roots of jungle trees. Subterranean tarantulas are usually plainly colored. *Citharischius crawshayi* is a uniform reddish brown while *Hysterocrates hercules* is plain beige.

Animals which are strongly dependent upon their subterranean lifestyle are barely able to move properly when removed from their burrows and placed on normal substrate. This is no surprise if one considers the "dachshund-like" legs of *C.*

Fig. 24. Entrance to the burrow of a trapdoor spider. After a heavy rain the spider leaves the door open to ventilate its "residence."

crawshayi. Very interesting spiders are those of the Harpactirinae. These animals, which occur in central and southern Africa (where they are known as monkey or baboon spiders) construct complicated systems of tunnels among leaf litter and partially underground. On their legs they have particularly well-developed adhesive pads which make them good climbers.

Obviously it is impossible to describe here all habitats of tarantulas. Because of the multiplicity of species of these creatures, the basic habitats described in this chapter present only a rough and superficial survey.

The Life of a Tarantula

Food

The main food of tarantulas are the large number and variety of insects which are available to them: grasshoppers, field crickets, house crickets and beetles are not only the most important foods in the wild, but also in the vivarium. Young tarantulas may be reared on the larvae of these insects.

Many authors are of the opinion that among tarantulas there are some specialist feeders. Although I would not attempt to divert our animals from a food which they prefer, I disagree with these authors. A tarantula which has been fed exclusively on beetles will also devour other insects after it has fasted for a while. I have not known this to harm them in any way.

Millipedes, that are often refused by other insects because of their foul-smelling secretions, will often be eaten with "relish" by tarantulas. During their nocturnal wanderings, some species of tarantulas, when hungry, will not refuse nestling mice, birds or even small reptiles. Other spiders, even those of the same species, may also be eaten. Above all, "spent" male tarantulas will be eaten by females to strengthen themselves before undertaking the arduous task of brood protection, a useful, and in no way gruesome arrangement of nature which helps to preserve the species.

Fig. 25. Prey is held between the chelicerae and is gradually crushed by kneading movements.

Hunting/Obtaining Food

While some species leave their refuges at dusk or during the night to hunt for prey, there are others that sit at the entrance to their tunnels to wait for prey passing by. These species, which spin very large webs in which they live, have a very small radius of activity. If their hunger is, however, too great, even they will leave their residence to actively hunt prey.

A spider's excellent sense of touch is especially evident while hunting prey. Even the slightest vibration caused by an insect moving causes the spider to turn in the direction of the insect in a fraction of a second. If the prey is within catching distance the spider uses all its strength to pounce upon it. It simultaneously pierces the insect with the fangs and, using chewing motions, attempts to kill it. If the prey puts up any resistance, it is firmly held by some or all of the legs. Prey which escapes will only be followed for a short distance.

It is rather astounding that some tarantulas do not immediately devour the prey that they have killed. Many species lay their prey to one side and then, using movements of their hind quarters, envelop it in silk. This creates a sort of carpet, in the center of which is the prey. Occasionally the prey is removed and the procedure of spinning repeated. To date, the purpose served by this procedure is unknown. Perhaps the contents of the spinning silk helps the food to digest better.

Feeding/Ingesting Food

Spiders have a stomach incomparable with that of any other animal. The feeding tube is so thin that only minute particles or liquids can pass through it. For this reason spiders are forced to liquefy their food outside the body—extraorally. This takes place by the animals producing secretions with complicated enzymes from their digestive tract and mixing it with their food. The enzymes dissolve the digestible particles of the food. By chewing movements of the chelicerae and other mandibular attachments, the food is squashed to a wet pulp from which the liquid nourishment is sucked into the stomach. By this means the abdomen may increase to double its volume.

After feeding only a small pellet of indigestible material remains between the chelicerae. This is deposited far away from where the animal lives. In this respect, the behavior of *Avicularia metallica* is quite amusing. It catapults its food remains in a wide arc up to 30 cm from the place where it lives.

Although only a very small amount of indigestible matter enters the stomach of a spider, the animal must also occasionally excrete waste. Waste products are stored in a special internal pocket and, when necessary, are disposed of. The waste products generally consist of fine guanine crystals of a whitish yellow color. When molested, *Acanthoscurria gigantea* will throw this excrement with great accuracy!

Growth

Tarantulas do not grow continually in the same way as humans, but rather in growth stages. Because the chitin shell cannot grow, the spider must from time to time molt the skin that has become too tight. Hormonal reactions initiate the molting process. Because of their higher metabolic rate, young spiders molt their skin every 2 to 3 weeks. Older animals molt after 2 or 3 months, while adult females molt at most once each year. Males do not molt again after the onset of sexual maturity.

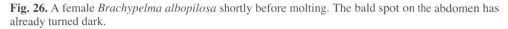

Fig. 26. A female *Brachypelma albopilosa* shortly before molting. The bald spot on the abdomen has already turned dark.

Several days to several weeks before molting, tarantulas cease feeding. At this time, their behavior is remarkably peaceful. I have even observed some animals undergo a sort of rest period or catalepsy. At this time, many spiders seek out dry, level places where they will sit for several days. Some species withdraw into their tunnels and seal the entrance from the inside. At this time they begin to cushion the chosen place with a very dense web; they construct a "molting carpet." Frequently New World species will rub off their abdominal hair and distribute it around the "molting carpet." Even the entrance to their residence is "spiked" with stinging hairs which effectively prevent small mammals from entering the tunnels.

It is at this time that under the old skin, hormonal processes are under way creating a new skin. If the molt is imminent an exuvial liquid is released between the two skins. On animals which have a "bald spot," this can be clearly seen. The original pink or flesh colored spot on the abdomen becomes almost black because the pigmentation of the new abdominal hairs has begun and light can no longer be reflected between the two layers of skin. The joints also become darker and the molt begins.

To achieve this, most species lie on their back on the "molting carpet." Some species, however, will begin the molt while lying on their stomach. There then follows a phase during which the animals lie motionless for many hours in order to conserve strength for the strenuous molting process. At this time, the bodily fluids are pressed from the abdomen into the fore quarters of the body. In this way the internal pressure in the body increases to double its original value. Flexing the chelicerae causes the carapace to split. It is first loosened from the old skin and then follows the extremities which are freed from the old skin by moving them rhythmically backwards and forwards. The easiest part of the molt is when the abdomen and the spinnerets emerge from the old skin because of the transfer of the liquid which the abdomen would usually contain. The cast-off skin (exuvia) is then raised in the air to fall to one side. The illustrations in Figs. 27–32 show these steps quite clearly.

The "fresh" spider then remains lying on its back for several hours while its chitinous shell begins to harden. When the legs are strong enough, the spider can then turn itself into its normal position. The hardening process takes at most a week after which the spider can then begin to hunt for prey again.

The molting process is one of the most dangerous periods in the life of a tarantula. If the spider is disturbed during molting, the process cannot continue in the normal manner. The animal remains trapped inside its old skin and dies. In the chapter "Frequent Errors in Tarantula Husbandry," I have dealt with possible causes of disturbance during molting in greater length.

Regeneration of Body Parts

If we examine a tarantula immediately after molting we can see that it has undergone several changes. The most obvious is that the colors have assumed their original intensity and that the body is once again completely covered by hair. In reality the ability of regeneration of tarantulas is one of the wonders of nature. Pedipalps, spinnerets, chelicerae and even two or three legs which the animal may have lost as the result of an accident are completely replaced after three or four molts.

Figs. 27 to 32. Various stages of molting of *Grammostola pulchripes*. The stages are described in the section on Growth.

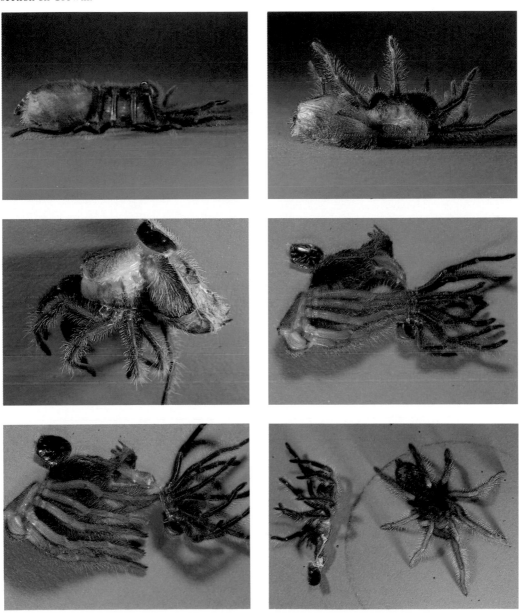

Fig. 33. A newly molted *Brachypelma auratum* beside its old skin.

Male tarantulas only molt until they are sexually mature. It is only after this molt (the imaginal molt) that the males' pedipalps develop bulbs at their ends. This is different from females which as a result of their longer life expectation—up to 25 years—must renew their worn external body parts each year. However, with each molt, females lose their spermatheca (seminal receptacle). Therefore females which are not mated after molting will not produce fertilized eggs.

Reproduction

Filling the Bulbs

Around 6 to 8 weeks after their maturity (imaginal) molt, male tarantulas become

Figs. 34 and 35. (above and below) *Brachypelma smithi* constructing a sperm web. (See also the following two pages).

extremely restless. The courtship and mating season has begun. First, however, the animals must fill the bulbs at the end of their pedipalps with sperm. To do this the male first spins a so-called sperm web, e.g., between two parallel branches or between the base and the side wall of the vivarium. The base is first covered with a dense layer of webbing which later serves as a platform for the male. A second, trapeze-shaped web is then spun at around 2–4 cm above and parallel to the platform. Finally, with a "forward roll" the male tarantula climbs between the two layers of web. The animal is now in a position—lying on its back—to deposit small drops of sperm from the genital region on the abdomen onto the underside of the upper web. Finally, the male crawls from between the layers of web and with its sternum above the upper web positions itself directly above the drops of sperm. With both pedipalps the male then reaches below the web and sucks up the drops of sperm by means of pumping actions of the bulbs. When this procedure is completed the male now destroys the useless sperm web, eating most of it. He is now ready to mate with a female.

Courtship and Mating

The courtship and mating rituals that follow vary from species to species. When attempting to attract a mate there are various

Figs. 34 and 35. (above and below) *Brachypelma smithi* constructing a sperm web. (See also the following two pages).

Figs. 36 and 37. When the web is completed, the animal does a "forward roll" below his web (Fig. 36). Fig. 37 shows a *Brachypelma emilia* lying on its back attaching drops of sperm to the web.

Finally, the spider crawls out, and standing upright, uses its pedipalps to reach below the net to suck the drops of sperm into the bulbs. The animal is now ready for copulation.

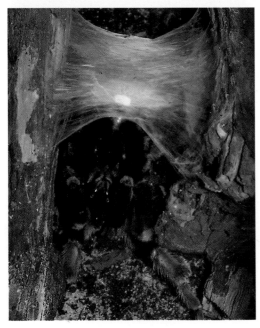

rhythmic head movements that are answered by the prospective partner. In the following I shall describe the courtship of *Brachypelma smithi,* the Mexican redknee tarantula which is protected by Appendix II of CITES but is commonly kept and easily bred in captivity. Even when no female is present, the male Mexican redknee tarantula will begin to search for a partner, usually at night. Standing upright on all eight legs he rhythmically contracts his leg muscles to produce a low frequency rumbling which is audible to the human ear. This lasts for around three seconds and is broken by four or five short pauses. If a female does not reply the noise is repeated after 15 or 20 seconds, often throughout the entire night. If there is a receptive female in the vicinity it usually answers the male. Around five seconds after the male's signal, the female produces a similar sound. The animals will often alternately stimulate one another for several hours. In the wild, the males will now approach the female's refuge, but in captivity the keeper must help by putting the male in the female's vivarium.

When the male is in the immediate vicinity of the female his behavior changes considerably. Producing the sound described above and by energetic drumming with the pedipalps and forelegs, the male attempts to attract the female's attention. While drumming, the

Fig. 38. Shows the same process with *Brachypelma smithi*.

male does not only use the ground but also the female's body.

I have observed some interesting behavior during attempts to mate.

Males court the previously quiet females with energetic drumming. This sound causes the female to suddenly become aggressive whereby she raises her body and spreads her chelicerae while shedding hair for a short time. When the female is in this position, the male spider has the perfect opportunity for copulation. Also at this time he is walking on a tightrope between life and death.

At this point the tibial hooks of the male come into action. He carefully pushes his

Fig. 39. *Phormictopus cancerides* mating.

forelegs between the chelicerae of the female. The tibial hooks anchor themselves in the chelicerae and keep the male at a safe distance. To a certain degree in a frontal position the male uses his pedipalps to fondle the female, first on the sternum and later in the genital region.

If the female is ready to copulate, she moves backwards giving the male the opportunity to insert the ends of his bulbs into her seminal receptacle. The often complicated shape of the bulbs sometimes forces the animals to twist their pedipalps to an amazing extent. One advantage, however, is the amazing flexibility of the bulbs.

It is interesting to note how the pairs separate after copulation. As opposed to orb web spiders, in the case of tarantulas it is only very rarely that the male is eaten after mating.

After copulation lasting—according to species—from 30 seconds (*Brachypelma smithi*) to 30 minutes, the female awakens from her copulatory trance and again becomes aggressive, or the male simply springs away to leave the female lying where she is.

It is only as males age after several copulations, that cannibalism may occur. After five or six matings, males lose the ability to send certain signals to females who then react in the same way as they would in the presence of any normal prey; the females bite. Males not ending up as food for females usually die soon after mating, even when in a separate vivarium. After their maturity (imaginal) molt the maximum life expectancy of a male is only around a year. This, however, is no reason for sorrow. If the males have been successful they have guaranteed that hundreds of descendants will come along to replace them.

Oviposition and Brood Protection

While the eggs are maturing in the female's abdomen, a process that takes 6 to 10 weeks, the animals begin to make prepara-

tions for oviposition. Here, too, there are species-specific patterns of behavior. For example *Brachypelma smithi* can usually be seen frequently throughout the year in the vivarium; when eggs are due they seek out a spacious tunnel for oviposition and spin a thick brooding chamber. Enthusiastic digging activity usually indicates impending oviposition. The animals will often turn their entire environment, i.e., the vivarium furnishings, upside down.

Fig. 40 shows *Brachypelma albopilosa* shortly before laying eggs. Inside a pear-shaped web the spider first spins a circular, bowl-shaped base for the eggs. This base will later form part of the eggsac. The female now presses her genital area to this base and deposits the eggs. Before the eggs actually leave the body they are fertilized through an opening in the receptacula seminis. The eggs are then enveloped in the same silk as that used for the construction of the base. The eggsac which is thus created is, however, still very flat. By using the pedipalps and cheliccrae to separate the base from the remainder of the brood chamber web the female creates a spherical shape. The still incomplete eggsac is then enveloped in a second layer of cotton-like silk which protects the eggs from the effects of the weather and cushions them against any external pressure. A third layer of silk, this time containing numerous stinging hairs, completes the

Fig. 40. *Brachypelma albopilosa* shortly before laying its eggs.

Fig. 41. An *Avicularia metallica* has already laid its eggs in a circular web and has covered them with more webbing. She now starts from the edge to loosen the clutch and form them into a perfect sphere.

Brachypelma smithi can become extremely aggressive.

Some species occasionally lay the eggsac on the ground to enable them to groom their body. When disturbed they will again pick it up with amazing speed. It is not true that tarantulas do not feed while protecting their brood. In my case, *Brachypelma smithi* ate several adult crickets during this period. Once the young have hatched they are guarded by the female for several days. After the first molt outside the eggsac they are able to feed for the first time. It is at this time that they disperse and their mother's protective behavior ceases.

Development of the Eggs

Before they become true young spiders, tarantulas go through several stages of development. The so-called nymphs hatch from their eggs after 2 to 3 weeks inside the eggsac. As they hatch the tiny, 3.5 mm pale yellow, almost motionless creatures also leave their embryonal skin so that one may speak of their first (neonate) molt. In build, they are still totally "underdeveloped" with the legs scarcely movable and the eyes only visible as small, round, black spots.

Within the first 6 weeks of life the nymphs molt for a second time and now

eggsac which by this time is almost completely spherical.

Tarantula females are perfect mothers. While the embryos (according to species, from 30 to 3000) are developing inside the eggs, they are carefully guarded by their owner. By carrying the eggsac between her chelicerae and pedipalps the female is also able to determine the climatic conditions under which the eggs will develop by placing the eggsac in a suitable place in her environment. If the female is molested she will first seek refuge by fleeing but if that does not succeed, some species, such as

Fig. 42. (above) A *Brachypelma albopilosa* with its eggsac.
Fig. 43. (below left) Development from egg to second larval stage. Animals in the second larval stage can leave the eggsac, but return in times of danger. After a further molt the animals are independent (Fig. 47) and can then feed themselves.
Fig. 44. (below right) Microphotograph of a nymph of *Brachypelma albopilosa* (× 20).

Fig. 45. View of an opened eggsac of *Grammostola pulchripes*. The young spiders are still in the second larval stage.

Fig. 46. The abdomen of larval *Theraphosa blondi* is almost as large as a pea.

begin to look like tarantulas. However, their movements are still severely limited. Legs and spinnerets are nevertheless functional, and the abdomen is slightly hairy. At this stage the spiderlings are able to survive without the protective eggsac. The previously light yellow animals now become darker. The abdomen turns black and around 14 days after the second molt the animals molt their skin for the third time. Three days after this molt they feed for the first time. The young are often a completely different color from their parents but change color over time. One of the main reasons for this is the temperature at which they are incubated e.g., as is the case for *Brachypelma albopilosa* which may be kept between 20 and 27 °C. At these temperatures, incubation takes between 7 and 12 weeks.

Husbandry and Breeding

Vivarium Construction

Even though the vivaria currently available commercially have been conceived for the husbandry of reptiles and amphibians, they are usually very impractical and poorly thought out, presenting a number of potentially fatal problems for tarantulas. One solution to this dilemma is to construct a suitable vivarium oneself. With easily available materials and a little skill one can quickly construct containers which will give pleasure for many years. Obviously, the construction of the small vivarium for tarantulas described in the following is only a suggestion which may be varied in a multitude of ways, but the basic requirements of the animals to be housed must be the first consideration.

Materials and Tools

- Sheets of 4 mm glass
- Silicon sealer (only acetate-based)
- Glass cutter
- Carborundum paper
- Plastic E-profile (track 4 mm glass)
- Perforated aluminum sheet (with holes of 1 to 2 mm) or crossweld wire mesh (mesh gauge 3–5 mm)
- Adhesive tape
- Fretsaw

The edges of all pieces of glass must be clean and smooth. Anyone using old recycled glass will be making savings in the wrong place. Inside the container there should be no gaps or crevices. It is here that the spiders' claws become trapped resulting in the loss of limbs. The height of the container for terrestrial and subterranean spiders should not be more than 30 cm because these animals often fall and the injuries may be fatal.

Fly mesh or other similar pliable materials as ventilation areas are totally unsuitable. The spiders often become trapped in this narrow mesh. To enable the vivarium to be easily serviced and cleaned, the front panel must be easy to remove. Anyone who already keeps tarantulas and must service their vivaria regularly can tell how irritating badly fit sliding doors and covers can be. Doors which slide horizontally in aluminum or plastic tracks often get jammed. The digging activities of the spiders causes grains of sand and small pieces of wood to get into the glass track. For photographing, for example, the vivarium should be easily accessible from both the front and from above. A cover can be easily made from aluminum T-profile.

To construct a vivarium measuring 30 × 20.8 × 20 cm (L × W × H) the following materials are needed:

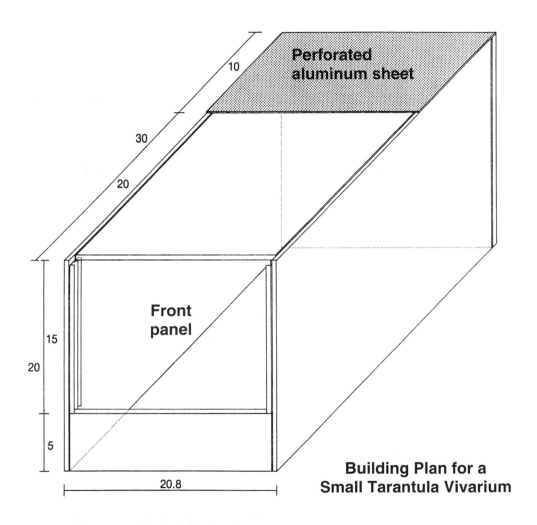

Perforated aluminum sheet

10

30

20

Front panel

15

20

5

20.8

Building Plan for a Small Tarantula Vivarium

- Base plate 20 × 30 cm (4 mm glass)
- Two side panels 30 × 20 cm (4 mm glass)
- Rear panel 20.8 × 20 cm (4 mm glass)
- Crosspiece 20 × 7 cm (4 mm glass)
- Cover 20 × 20 cm
- Perforated aluminum sheet 20.8 × 10 cm for ventilation
- Two pieces of plastic E-profile 13 cm
- Front panel (4 mm glass)

The first step is to affix one of the side panes and the rear pane to the outside of the base plate. These panes should be held in position by adhesive tape. After this, the other side pane and the crosspiece should be fixed in position. When 12 hours have elapsed to allow the silicon sealer to harden, the top should be fixed between the two side panes. At this point it should be mentioned that the top should be pushed back 4.5 mm. The gap thus created accommodates the front pane. The ventilation sheet should be affixed to the rear of the cover at this time. Finally, the two pieces of plastic E-profile which guide the front panel should be installed. The dimensions of the front panel can only be accurately measured when the remainder of the vivarium is completed.

Vivaria of this size may be neatly stacked in a shelving unit 30 cm deep. In such a shelving unit 1.20 m long and 0.80 m high, I store 15 tarantula vivaria and their lighting equipment quite comfortably.

Vivaria for Avicularinae should be built in the same way with the dimensions increased to the appropriate heights, e.g., 30 × 30 × 50 cm (L × W × H).

Furnishings

The well-being of a tarantula depends largely upon the furnishings in its vivarium. Even the smallest amount of unsuitable objects or smallest degree of unsuitable conditions can cause the animals to wander around the vivarium aimlessly for several hours. They will often use their chelicerae to attempt to find a way out via the ventilation plate. In this way they exert themselves to the extreme and accidents are unavoidable. The fangs break off and the animals are no longer able to feed. When furnishing a vivarium, the following basic guidelines should be observed:

1) The animals must have access to moist as well as completely dry places.
2) All constructions (refuges, caves etc.) should be built in such a way that they cannot collapse when the spider is digging.
3) Under no circumstances should sharp or pointed objects be placed in the vivarium (e.g., broken rocks, cacti and other succulents with spines).
4) Condensation on the sides of the vivarium will cause the spiders to slip when climbing. By fixing small pieces of tree bark to the sides (using only silicon sealer) this danger is removed.
5) Use only natural materials such as earthenware, ceramics, peat, bark etc. Great care should be taken when cork products are used, especially those intended for the building industry! They are impregnated and contain binding materials which are usually poisonous to spiders. Potting compost containing weed-killer should also not be used.

Fig. 49. A shelved arrangement suitable for housing large numbers of tarantulas.

Fig. 50. This vivarium has been furnished to house arboreal tarantulas from rain forests.

6) Plants should only be installed after they have been thoroughly rinsed five or six times within 14 days. Fresh plants (especially those which have been bought very cheaply) are often poisoned with insecticides.

7) If pure sand or gravel is used as substrate even the most robust tarantula will die fairly quickly. These materials together with food and excrement are the ideal breeding ground for harmful bacteria, fungi and mites.

8) To allow insects to escape from them, the drinking bowls should contain rocks that protrude from the water.

The possibilities of furnishing a tarantula vivarium are enormous and range from a simple steppe vivarium for spiders from dry regions to magnificent paludaria with luxuriant tropical plants. Fig. 50 shows a small vivarium (60 × 40 × 40 cm) in which I have kept *Avicularia metallica* and some African giant millipedes for several years. One aspect of tarantula husbandry, however, cannot be ignored: The larger and more attractively furnished the vivarium the less frequently the animals will be seen.

Types of Vivaria

Vivarium for Terrestrial Tarantulas

The substrate should be 5–8 cm deep and should consist of potting compost normally available commercially or a peat/sand mixture (¾ peat). In vivaria less than 40 cm it is not worth installing plants. The spiders will quickly become accustomed to this arrangement. A flat piece of bark should be placed in a dark place in the vivarium. This will be especially appreciated by the genus *Brachypelma*. Many species will favor this place for molting. An artificial cave in the form of a piece of curved cork bark should be placed in another position in the vivarium. This may be obtained in any pet shop. A halved, earthenware plant pot is equally suitable. A small drinking bowl completes this spartan but perfectly functional arrangement for tarantulas. In larger vivaria a piece of tree trunk may be half-buried in the substrate. If this is done the other objects mentioned above become superfluous because the spider will construct its own refuge.

Vivarium for Subterranean Tarantulas

The most suitable containers for these animals are the all-glass aquaria normally available commercially—naturally with a well-fitting cover. If this is filled to two-thirds of its depth with a substrate of garden soil or loam it will meet all the requirements of its occupant. To be able to watch and observe the animals, a piece of half-round cork bark should be inserted into the substrate in such a way that the open side is against the front panel and only the open end protrudes from above the substrate. The front panel should then be covered with black paper which may be removed to watch the animals or check on their well-being. A small drinking bowl is indispensable.

Vivarium for Arboreal Tarantulas

These vivaria can be attractively furnished. Because arboreal species rarely come to the ground, many materials may be used as substrate. Especially suitable is a shallow layer of peat covered with a layer of moss.

The clay balls used in hydroponic plant culture may also be used.

Climbing branches are, of course, essential for arboreal species. A few branches with twigs are adequate for most species. It is imperative that the rear and side walls of these vivaria be covered with tree bark. The spiders will not damage any plants which are installed. In the vivarium the plants will also provide a climate which is comfortable and beneficial for the spiders. Plants will only thrive in larger containers and must be serviced daily. Lighting is also indispensable and only fluorescent lights should be used. In my experience I have found the following plants to be suitable for these vivaria:

Maranta leuconora; high humidity, moist substrate, much light, temperature up to 27 °C.

Scindapsus sp.; high humidity, semi-moist substrate, medium light, temperature up to 25 °C.

Philodendron scandens; medium humidity, moist substrate, low light, temperature up to 23 °C.

Ficus repens (synonym *F. pumilio*); low humidity, moist substrate, much light, up to 27 °C.

Hoya caya; dry air, slightly moist-substrate, much light, up to 24 °C.

Syngonium sp.; very high atmospheric humidity, moist substrate, much light, up to 27 °C.

Diseases and Natural Enemies

An unpleasant chapter to write deals with the diseases of our charges. Essentially, most diseases have not yet been researched and that would appear to be the case for the foreseeable future. There are no medications which will help to cure the diseases of tarantulas.

Medicines intended for human and veterinary purposes are completely useless and will only make the condition of an ill spider even worse. It is, therefore, essential to know how to cure a spider should it become ill. From my own experiences I shall now describe some frequent diseases and their treatment.

Fungal Infections

If kept in poor conditions even the most healthy tarantula will fall victim to a fungal infection. If the conditions are too moist or there is insufficient ventilation, this allows the fungal spores to establish themselves on the body of the spider. The first infection is usually found on the patellae and the cephalothorax. It then spreads quickly over the entire body of the spider. The spores will especially seek out sites of injury.

Fungal infection is easily recognized. The initially small white or gray spots become much larger within two to three

Fig. 51. *Melopoeus minax* (new taxonomy: *Haplopelma minax*) with a fungal infection on the carapace.

weeks. If this infection is not immediately treated the chitinous skin of the spider will quickly be damaged, especially on the legs. This makes them very susceptible to other diseases. The metabolic products of the fungus poison the spider. Infected spiders initially behave normally but after a short time they lie apathetically in a corner of the vivarium. Finally, they will no longer react to any disturbance.

Removing the animals to a clean and newly furnished vivarium with better ventilation will help to improve the situation. Painting the infected parts with isopropyl (alcohol from a pharmacy) has proven to have a positive effect. Afterwards the parts painted with this solution should be dried with blotting paper or cotton. Fig. 51 shows a *Haplopelma* species with a fungally infected carapace. After painting with isopropyl and the subsequent molt the animal was once more completely clean.

Fig. 52. The glassy appearance at the rear of the body of *Brachypelma smithi* is probably the result of a viral infection. The three dark brown flecks are also abnormal. The animal was photographed soon after death.

Bacteria and Viruses

It is almost hopeless to attempt to battle against an illness caused by bacteria or viruses. Sadly, the illnesses caused by these organisms are quite frequent and their causes often can not be recognized. Most often, the causes of illness are unhygenic conditions and incorrect husbandry.

One illness is shown by Fig. 52. Small, round, lens-shaped blisters filled with liquid often form on the abdomen (especially in very old animals). These are similar to the blisters which form when human skin is burned, and are particularly easy to recognize when they occur in urticating spiders. The initially small area gradually increases in size and within 4 weeks usually covers the entire surface of the abdomen. The hindquarters now appear glassy and swollen. Blackish-brown flecks appear on the surface of the skin. That is the final stage of the disease, and the spider dies. These diseases can only be prevented by providing our charges with optimum vivarium conditions.

Parasites

Tarantulas, especially those taken from the wild, are often infected by parasites. A case of parasitic mites is easy to see because they sit on the skin of the spider's joints. Fig. 16 shows a scorpion with a severe infestation of mite larvae. When a spider's skin is perforated by the sucking of mites it allows disease-causing organisms to enter the spider's body. An infected spider must be carefully watched. When the spider changes its position the mites can be easily crushed with very small forceps. Never to try to remove a mite that is firmly attached to the spider!

Colonies of mites between the chelicerae usually live symbiotically with the spider. They feed on particles of waste food and keep the spider's chelicerae clean. In return, the spider provides protection and food. If, however, the number of mites becomes too large, they are best removed using a fine artist's brush. Under normal circumstances the number of mites decreases on tarantulas kept in the vivarium.

Much more serious and inevitably fatal is an infestation of nematodes. These millimeter-long worms occur almost everywhere in nature. In some spiders the reproductive rate of these organisms may only be described as explosive. A female *Brachypelma,* which initially appeared quite normal, suddenly lost both pedipalps. From the resultant wounds were small worms, many thousands of which were subsequently found in the pedipalps and the head portion of the cephalothorax. After 2 days the spider died, having been devoured from within by these worms.

Open wounds on newly imported spiders are usually covered with the eggs or larvae of small species of flies. The eggs quickly hatch, also producing larvae which penetrate inside the spider and cause great damage. It is imperative that spiders injured in this way are kept in quarantine.

Tarantula Wasps

In the wild there is an interesting form of parasitism between spiders and certain species of wasps. Wasps of the genus *Pepsis* specialize on various species of tarantulas. The vagabond female wasps seek out tarantulas and their refuges in typical spider biotopes. If the female wasp finds a spider of a certain species it attempts to inflict an immobilizing sting. If this is successful the spider is trapped in its self-excavated refuge, which allows the wasp to attach one or more eggs to the spider's body. When they hatch, these eggs produce larvae which eat into the immobilized spider. During the course of a few weeks they first consume all smaller, less important parts of the spider and then go on to consume all vital internal organs. The spider is alive during this time. The larvae finally pupate outside the dead spider. Two weeks after pupation a new wasp hatches, and the entire process begins once more.

In addition to wasps, small mammals and birds are also the natural enemies of tarantulas. Young spiders are also often found in the stomachs of reptiles and amphibians.

Injuries

Compared with the diseases mentioned above, in the case of injuries good "first aid" can often be given. Injuries are often caused when the animals are being caught, transported or during attempts at mating. Even in an optimally furnished vivarium accidents may sometimes occur. Below is a list of suggestions of what to do in such cases.

Injuries to the Limbs

When attempting to climb, well-nourished ground-dwelling spiders will often tear off an entire limb or pedipalp or part thereof. In general, the loss of a whole leg is not so tragic. On their coxae, tarantulas have naturally occurring fracture planes which allow them to detach their limbs in times of emergency. The wound thus caused heals quickly. It is more severe, however, when the limbs break at other positions: the wound will not heal by itself. Each time the spider moves, large amounts of body fluids ooze from the wound and in this case, the remainder of the limb must be amputated. Using long forceps, the ends of which are covered by rigid tubing (air tubing used for aquaria), one should take a firm hold of the middle of the femur of the injured leg. By gradually increasing the pressure one forces the spider to disconnect the remainder of the injured limb. Usually the spider will put up energetic resistance to this procedure. Once held, the grip on the leg must not be loosened. Often a loud cracking noise will be heard as the remainder of the limb is discarded. Another way to remove the remainder of a damaged limb is by means of a noose. A noose of cotton—or fine knitting wool—is placed around the femur of the damaged leg. By a sharp tug on each end of the noose the leg will normally be discarded.

Injuries to the Chelicerae and Cephalothorax

Tarantulas, especially aggressive species, will occasionally lose one of their fangs. Their hunting ability is thus strictly limited, and they should only be given soft foods such as newly molted insects. After the next molt the damaged parts will be renewed.

Animals which lose both fangs simultaneously have almost no hope of survival and usually die of starvation.

Injuries to the cephalothorax are usually healed following one or two molts. Figs. 51 and 117 show such an injured and subsequently healed animal. Small punctures of the abdomen usually heal without any problems. Larger wounds such as cuts or splits inevitably lead to great losses of bodily liquids and are not able to be healed. To prevent a long and agonizing death it is best to euthanize the spider by freezing it quickly.

Broken pedipalps have no adverse effect on a tarantula and if the wound is not oozing, amputation is not necessary.

Husbandry of Tarantulas in the Vivarium

Tarantulas are particularly undemanding charges. However, that does not mean that they may be neglected. Some animals require almost no care. Nevertheless, anyone who has ever reared around 100 young tarantulas can tell how labor intensive this hobby can become.

Routine Tasks

As well as a daily visual check on the animals, every 2 days the water bowls must be removed, cleaned and replenished with fresh water. In the case of tarantulas from moist, tropical regions the humidity level of the substrate should be regularly checked and when necessary adjusted by spraying or watering. Spiders should not be sprayed directly. Many species will panic and may injure themselves.

Either weekly or fortnightly, the glass panels of the vivaria should be cleaned of webs and excrement. Do not use any detergents! Clean, warm water is usually sufficient. If the panels to be cleaned can be removed they may be washed in warm soapy water but must be thoroughly rinsed before being replaced in the vivaria. Spiders usually deposit food remnants in a certain place in the vivaria. This may be removed with long forceps as may any remnants of molted skin. Overgrown plants may also be pruned at this time. If several animals are kept, records of molting, mating, injuries and so forth should be kept in a card file.

At intervals of at most a year, the vivaria must be completely cleaned. At this time the tarantula should be placed in a newly furnished vivarium. The soiled vivarium should then be emptied, thoroughly cleaned and filled to the correct depth with new substrate. Furnishings may be washed with warm water and reused.

Spiders wandering ceaselessly around the vivarium are not comfortable in their surroundings. Placing the animals in another container will often help the situation.

It is astounding how little work is involved when keeping only one tarantula: they require around 30 minutes of work weekly, and are far less demanding than other vivarium animals. Nevertheless if the number of animals kept increases, so does the amount of work involved and a means of time saving is called for, such as storing the vivaria on a shelving unit described earlier. Naturally the incidental running costs also increase and one may reckon with a cost of around $3.00 per week per animal.

Frequent Errors in Tarantula Husbandry

The husbandry of tarantulas also requires a little intelligence on the part of their owners. Like someone who keeps reptiles and amphibians, tarantula keepers must first gain expert knowledge and experience of their animals, their habits and behavior.

Although most frequently kept tarantulas hail from tropical and subtropical regions, many arachnologists keep their animals in temperatures that are too high. Fatalities during and after molting are usually the result, with the animals dying without showing any outward signs of discomfort. Temperatures between 25 and 28 °C are quite adequate for most species. Arboreal species prefer slightly higher temperatures.

If conditions are too dry (in a centrally heated home) this can prolong the essential molting process in many species. Signs of this are the spider's colors becoming pale or the animal becoming listless. The same signs may be seen if the animals are kept under conditions that are too cold or too moist.

I have already mentioned the danger of injuries in the chapter "Vivarium Construction." The cause of many injuries is food insects remaining in the vivarium. House and field crickets will happily begin to eat a spider while it is molting. Any uneaten food should be removed from the vivarium after a few hours.

If cats or dogs are kept in the same household under no circumstances should flea collars, flea powder or other insecticides be used. Insect sprays, mosquito sprays, Mafu Strips™, mothballs, Vapona Strips™ and so forth will bring "guaranteed death" to tarantulas even if they are used in another room. Cleaning materials containing ammonia can also have a harmful effect on spiders over a long period.

It is also senseless to allow tarantulas to "exercise" in the apartment. Apart from the obvious dangers this presents, it also means that the animal has to reorient itself in its vivarium. This can also interrupt the natural chain of behavior such as mating, oviposition, brood protection and molting which all have a negative effect on the well-being of the animal.

Correct Feeding

The well-being of tarantulas depends to a large extent upon feeding them correctly. Badly fed animals will grow slowly, molt badly and cannot be expected to lay eggs. Moreover, the growth of males will be greatly retarded, and they'll rarely be able to mate with females. When feeding, it is not merely a case of offering a varied diet, but more a case of when, how and how often food should be given.

Young spiders should be given food of the appropriate size every 2 to 3 days. Babies are best fed on *Drosophila* and newly

hatched field and house crickets. After five or six molts they will be able to take small houseflies and crickets up to 7 mm long. To feed extremely small and sensitive baby spiders, a "trick" should be mentioned.

Most spiders will eat freshly killed food. A supply of minute food insects may be kept in the freezer for some time. If a number of thawed insects are placed near the young spiders at night they will usually be quickly located and eaten. Food insects which have grown too large may also be presented to young spiders in the same way. Once they have reached a size of around 2 cm, young spiders are quite capable of devouring adult crickets.

The danger of spiders being eaten by food insects is especially great in the case of young spiders because they molt at relatively short intervals. In these cases it is even more important to remove food from the vivarium.

Adult tarantulas should be offered food every 7 to 14 days. To prevent excess food being left in the vivarium an individual cricket should be presented in forceps to determine if the spider is hungry. If the cricket is immediately seized a further four or five may be released into the vivarium.

Occasionally male tarantulas will shy away from crickets. Their hopping makes the spiders nervous. In such cases, the rear legs of the crickets should be removed. The same method should be used with spiders with a full, distended abdomen because the hind legs of the crickets can easily damage the abdomen of the spiders.

Newly imported spiders are often badly undernourished. To be able to persuade them to take a large amount of food in a short time, use their usual readiness to accept newly killed food. Cubes of beef heart of 1.5 cm will usually also be gratefully accepted by these starved creatures. Any unconsumed meat should be removed after 36 hours.

As already mentioned in the general section, insects form the main part of the diet of tarantulas. Because the variety of insects available for use in the vivarium has increased enormously in recent years, mealworms are now hardly ever used. These have been replaced by much better quality insects such as field crickets, house crickets, locusts, houseflies, black beetle larvae, waxworms, cockroach larvae etc. Only on rare occasions should large spiders be given baby mice. By using the food animals mentioned above the entire diet of tarantulas can be supplied. My tarantulas are fed exclusively on field and house crickets and enjoy perfect health. At the same time considerable expense can be spared if only one sort of food is used.

Purchase and Breeding of Food Animals

All food animals mentioned earlier may be bought from any reliable pet shop throughout the year. Crickets are without doubt the most economical foods. It is also possible to order these foods direct from the breeder to be delivered to your door every 7 to 14 days and in the desired amounts.

Food insects must also be properly cared for. They should have a vivarium suitably furnished for them and should be given the correct food. This, in the long term, saves money and greatly increases their value as food for the tarantulas.

Anyone with sufficient space may also breed tarantula food quite easily. This is by far the most economical method. One should, however, remember that breeding food insects takes time. There is adequate literature available about breeding food insects so we do not need to go into this subject in this volume.

Correct Handling of Tarantulas

Keeping tarantulas does not only require knowledge of the animals themselves but also how they should be handled, packed, transported and so forth. The worst mistakes are usually made with regard to packing and transport.

Handling

Basically tarantulas should be handled as little as possible. Only when absolutely necessary should peaceful and calmer species such as *Brachypelma* and *Avicularia* be taken from the vivarium by hand. In doing so they should not be tightly gripped but should first be allowed to walk onto the palm of the hand. They may be gently nudged along with a finger.

To be able to check the sex of young spiders one must be able to inspect the underside of the abdomen. To do this the thumb and forefinger should be placed between the second and third pair of legs to hold the cephalothorax. If the spiders become restless they should be released immediately to prevent injury. Aggressive and fast-moving animals should never be touched with the hands. They may be easily moved and inspected by placing a transparent plastic container over them and a sheet of transparent plastic beneath them.

Forceps and similar instruments should never be used to handle tarantulas. Because of the pressure these instruments can exert on the cephalothorax they can cause internal injuries.

Packing for Shipment

Anyone becoming intensively occupied with spiders will soon face the task of having to send captive bred young or adults over long distances. If one intends to transport the creatures oneself, they may be simply carried in small plastic aquaria. However, during cold weather, it is advisable to protect the animals by using styrofoam boxes. The postal service will transport these shipments. Here are a few tips for this method of transport.

The main prerequisite for safe postal transport is adequate packing and here no false savings should be made. The most suitable containers are rigid styrofoam boxes with tight-fitting covers—cardboard cartons may get crushed in transit. Air holes are not necessary and will reduce the insulating effect of the styrofoam. Spiders should be placed individually in transparent containers filled with shredded paper towel, leaving only sufficient space for the spider. The shredded paper will cushion the spider and provide it with a secure foothold. If the container is too large the spiders will be shaken about during transport and injured.

Under no circumstances should food or moist foam rubber be placed in the container with the spider. The water will adhere to the entire abdomen of the spider and present the danger of suffocation. Naturally, tarantulas should not be dispatched shortly before molting. Ventilation holes in the transparent plastic con-

tainers will encourage the spiders to attempt to escape and could result in the
fangs breaking off.

The styrofoam box containing the transparent containers should be filled to the rim
with crumpled newspaper or excelsior
which has not been treated with pesticides,
and the cover fitted and firmly taped.

The package may be sent "Express De-
livery" and will arrive very quickly, perhaps within 12 hours. If the temperature
falls below 15 °C (think also of the final
destination) the package should not be sent
by mail.

Neutral, unidentifiable packing will also
ease the transport of the package by mail.
The mail will undertake the transport of
vertebrate animals only under certain conditions: no air holes and no label "LIVE
ANIMALS" on the package. However,
when sending spiders by mail, these requirements do not apply.

Breeding Tarantulas

When keeping tarantulas, one of the most
important objectives of the hobby is to try
to breed them. This helps to reduce the
number of wild-caught imports and helps
to supply other interested parties with
healthy specimens. Among enthusiasts it is
quite common for various species of young
spiders to be exchanged.

Selection of Breeding Stock

With immature spiders it is difficult to dis-
tinguish the sexual differences. Before the
adult molt the sexes of most species appear
to be identical. There is, however, one
characteristic which allows the sexes to be
distinguished with 70% certainty: on the
abdominal underside above the epigastric
furrow, males have a round, dark area of
0.5 to 2 mm in diameter. This is the spinning gland area which comes into action
later while the male spins the sperm web.
The genital opening of the males is surrounded by two tufts of fine hair.

In females, the genital opening in the
epigastric furrow may be up to 7 mm wide.
From around the fifth molt, males may be
distinguished in this way. A strong magnifying glass will considerably simplify ob-
servation. Figs. 53 and 54 show the genital
areas of *Aphonopelma chalcodes*.

Frequently, newly caught spiders will
spin an eggsac in their new container. If
young emerge from this, one is able to start
breeding them in 2 or 3 years. At this age,
the males of most species are sexually mature, and the original sexually mature female is already available.

Breeding Groups

How should a breeding group be composed?
The smallest possible breeding group is an

Figs. 53 and 54. (above and below) In sub-adult male tarantulas there is a dark, circular area above the epigastral groove. Fig. 53 shows a female *Aphonopelma chalcodes* and Fig. 54 shows a sub-adult male of the same species.

individual pair. Such an arrangement, however, has considerable disadvantages: if no young are produced, one is left with only a female. In the meantime, the male will have long since died. If one has the opportunity to select several animals, it is best to proceed in the following manner: one to three females and three to five males of various sizes and ages to allow one the opportunity to carry out mating attempts during the following years. Females are not all receptive at the same time, and with several animals numerous mating combinations may be attempted.

Tarantula males have a very short lifespan during which they are only able to mate for a very short period. With a number of animals of different ages, each year one of the males will become sexually mature. Thus "fresh" males are regularly available.

Over time, my initial breeding group of 15 *B. smithi* has been reduced to 8 animals. The seven males became sexually mature over a period of 4 years. If one has only young animals (after two or three molts) a variety of "tricks" must be tried to establish pairs.

Although female spiders may take around 4 to 6 years to attain sexual maturity, males of the same species may be sexually mature after only 2 or 3 years. When kept under different conditions, young spiders can also grow at different rates. If fe-

male spiders are reared under optimum conditions while males are reared "on a back burner," with a little luck, sexually mature partners will be obtained at the same time. However, this method will only work with a few species. I have bred *Brachypelma vagans* using this method, but had no success using it on *Grammostola spatulata*. In the case of the latter species, the males were sexually mature after 2 years although they barely measured 4 cm!

Aggression Between Sexes

The patterns of behavior between the sexes varies within individual species. Although some exhibit extremely peaceful courtship behavior, others become almost frantic. Even species which may normally be handled with impunity and without hesitation can become extremely aggressive toward their partners both during and after mating. After mating, *Brachypelma smithi* females will regularly attempt to kill their partners by biting. In total contrast, however, *Theraphosa blondi,* a normally aggressive species is "as gentle as a lamb" during mating.

After initial nervous stridulation the female, if she is receptive, will allow the male to mate without any signs of aggression. The subsequent separation of the sexes is equally peaceful. Many males of the genera *Haplopelma* and *Selenocosmia,* however, can only find safety by fleeing from the female after mating. For mating, these species should, therefore, be given as much space as possible since the male will inevitably be sought out and killed by the female. Some species of the genus *Avicularia* are extremely peaceful during the breeding season. An adult pair of *Avicularia metallica* lived together peacefully for over 10 months in a vivarium of 30 × 30 × 20 cm (L × W × H)! Nevertheless, in general I prefer to assume that before, during and after mating most species of tarantulas behave very aggressively toward their partner; although with healthy, vigorous animals, fatalities rarely occur. Naturally, however, there are exceptions!

Introducing a Pair

Pairs may be introduced in a number of ways. In some species, the males are extremely "sensitive"; the slightest sign of trouble will cause them to cease mating behavior. I have observed this with almost all non-American and aggressive species of the genera *Poecilotheria, Ceratogyrus, Harpactira, Pterinochilus* and *Hysterocrates,* and also some American species of *Aphonopelma, Brachypelma, Crypsidro-*

mus and *Acanthoscurria.* With these species it is best to place the female in the vivarium containing the courting male, but this must be done very calmly and carefully.

With less sensitive animals such as *Brachypelma albopilosum, Brachypelma vagans* and *Grammostola* species, both sexes may be removed from their vivaria and placed together for mating.

It is, however, much more difficult to induce copulation in species where both sexes behave very aggressively toward one another. These animals include all species of the genera *Haplopelma* and *Selenocosmia.* At the slightest disturbance, these animals react very quickly. Neither sex is suitable for removal from its own vivarium for direct introduction to its partner. In this case it has proved expedient to place both sexes in the same vivarium at the same time but separated by wire mesh. If courtship behavior between the spiders is observed during the night, the wire mesh should be slowly and very carefully removed.

To protect the partners from injuring one another, the keeper should arm himself with a wooden rod, or even better, a laboratory glass rod. If the animals should attempt to bite one another, the rod should be placed between the female's chelicerae, and the animals should be separated. Here, extreme caution is advised. When trying to escape, some species of spiders (*Haplopelma, Ceratogyrus*) can climb the rod very quickly.

To prevent himself from being bitten on the hand or arm, the keeper should smear the glass rod with glycerine (from a drugstore) before the animals are introduced. The spiders will no longer be able to climb the glass rod and instead will slide down.

Data on courtship, sperm web construction, copulation, oviposition and so on should be carefully recorded. During mating the spiders should be constantly watched and anything which could disturb the spiders should be removed.

After successful copulation when the male has inserted his palps into the female's genital opening several times, the animals should be replaced in their own vivaria. Within a week, healthy, strong males will construct a new sperm web after which they may again be used for further matings.

If after 6 to 8 weeks after copulation females of terrestrial species are seen to be digging more frequently than usual, this is a sign that eggs will soon follow. At this time the vivarium, if it is illuminated, should be darkened. While producing the eggsac the female is extremely sensitive. Under no circumstances should they be disturbed; otherwise incubation will be interrupted and problems will occur.

Incubation of the Eggsac

If breeding is allowed to proceed under natural conditions, the eggsac is left in the vivarium to be reared by the female who will guard it and regularly move it to other parts of the vivarium for temperature or humidity regulation. This method does, however, present certain risks. Mites or springtails, which are inevitably present in a tarantula vivarium, could enter the eggsac and damage the eggs. Newly hatched crickets may also damage the eggsac. If disturbed too often, females may neglect the eggsac. If temperature fluctuates too much, the development of the eggs could become protracted, tempting the spider to eat the eggsac.

Less risky, but also more labor intensive, is to incubate the eggsac under artificial conditions. The eggsac should be removed from the female and placed in a separate container in which a thermostat is used to keep the temperature constant day and night. It is very important that the eggsac does not come into contact with condensation. This would cause the eggs to mold. Moist earth in the incubation container ensures that the atmospheric humidity is always adequately high. A sloping cover will prevent condensation from falling onto the eggsac. During incubation the eggsac should be frequently turned to prevent the eggs or spiderlings on the bot-

Fig. 55. This young *Pamphobeteus* species is still attractively colored. After the sixth molt the animal will be a uniform dark brown.

tom from being crushed. Using one or two needles, the eggsac may also be suspended from a piece of wood or could be placed on a small piece of plastic mesh. It must not, however, come into contact with the substrate.

Using the last method, the development of the eggs may be carefully watched. Using sharp scissors, the eggsac should be carefully opened. Beforehand, some petri dishes (from a laboratory) should have been sterilized by heating in an electric oven for an hour at 200 °C. Disinfectant must not be used! The petri dishes should be lined with surgical cellulose which has been moistened with a few drops of water. Each petri dish should be opened, and eggs from the eggsac should be placed in it. A 10 cm diameter petri dish is large enough for 50 to 100 eggs. The petri dishes should be placed in a darkened container with a constant temperature. During regular checks of the petri dishes, it is easy to remove dead or moldy eggs with forceps.

When breeding tarantulas, I prefer to use the first method described above, and only when the female behaves abnormally and neglects the eggsac do I use the petri dish method.

To check the condition of eggs or babies in an eggsac, small, fine scissors should be used to make a small slit in its wall. Using two pairs of forceps the slit may be opened making it possible to check the contents of the eggsac.

After checking the contents, the hole should be held closed with a pair of flat forceps while a second person sews the edges together with very fine sewing thread. After this procedure, the eggsac may be returned to the female spider.

As soon as the young spiders leave the eggsac and feed voluntarily after their first molt, they should be placed in individual, small plastic containers, each holding a layer of peat or potting compost. Moist, surgical cotton is less suitable because this quickly becomes dirty.

The first food given to young spiders should be newly hatched field and house crickets and adult *Drosophila*. For the smallest young spiders, one must breed springtails. The young of some *Metriopelma* species will even sometimes retreat from *Drosophila melanogaster*!

Obtaining Tarantulas

The first and most obvious way to purchase a tarantula is by visiting the local pet shop where one might find a number of species.

Often, imported spiders are in bad condition because they are usually transported in several stages, frequently causing them to starve and thirst for up to 3 months. If such specimens do not die during transport, they usually do so after only a short time at the dealer's premises.

It is simple to determine if a tarantula is healthy:

– When disturbed, they will immediately assume a defensive posture.
– Animals with a very small or wrinkled abdomen will immediately seize a cricket when it is presented.
– The limbs must not be bent or folded beneath the front of the body.
– Extremely large specimens are usually very old females; for a beginner medium-sized animals are better.

– When the spider moves, there should be no liquid oozing from the skin over the joints. This is a certain sign that the animals have been too dry for too long during transport and can no longer be saved.
– The fangs must not hang down loosely.
– The abdomen must be symmetrically shaped without pustules, spots or blisters.
– If small or medium-sized specimens have legs missing, it is not necessarily serious.

Anyone who has kept or may even have bred tarantulas will inevitably have contact with other tarantula keepers. This enables the enthusiasts to exchange captive-bred young among themselves.

This is without doubt the most interesting way to obtain tarantulas and enables the enthusiast to build up a varied collection in a relatively short amount of time.

Nowadays, large numbers of a variety of tarantula species are regularly bred in captivity so that fewer wild-caught animals need to be imported. Some regularly bred tarantula species are listed below:

Avicularia metallica
Brachypelma albopilosa
Brachypelma vagans
Psalmopoeus cambridgei
Grammostola spatulata

Less commonly bred species include the following:

Theraphosa blondi
Avicularia avicularia
Metriopelma species
Selenocosmia species
Ceratogyrus species
Harpactira species

The desire to own large, adult tarantulas is understandably great, but one should remember that captive-bred spiders also grow very quickly and cost only a fraction of the prices demanded for adult specimens.

Anyone who is able to obtain captive-bred young from private breeders or institutions usually does not need to worry about the health of the spiders.

The dream of every arachnologist, however, is to travel to the home of his animals where the habitats may be studied and animals for his use may be caught. Nevertheless, finding the biotopes does require a certain amount of experience. It is quite common for a collector to return home empty-handed but great surprises are also possible. While in Costa Rica hunting for *Aphonopelma seemanni* in untouched natural areas, some collectors were surprised that there were almost no spiders of this species to be found. The collectors were, however, amazed to find that in a sheep meadow on a sloping hillside not far from their hotel they discovered dozens of tunnels of this species. In other areas,

Aphonopelma seemanni was also only found in similar habitats.

Methods of catching spiders are also becoming more ingenious. Previously the animals were simply dug up, nowadays one makes use of their behavior and habits. Many species have an inborn fear of water; thus if water is carefully poured down the side of their burrows, it will not take long before the spider appears at the entrance. Using a long, rigid piece of wood the spider's return passage is then blocked. What sounds so simple here, however, requires a great deal of experience and dexterity.

With aggressive species, use can be made of their constant readiness to bite: a long piece of fine wire, one end of which is bent to form a 1–2 cm circle and then covered with a 2 cm ball of candle wax, is carefully inserted into the spider's tunnel. Usually, the spider, which is rather "irate" at this intrusion, will immediately bite into the wax ball. While angling, the wire should be kept taut. The spider is not able to release its fangs from the wax quickly and can thus be carefully pulled from its tunnel. Naturally this method is only successful if the tunnels are relatively straight and short.

Prevention of Accidents

Although in general there is no great danger from tarantulas, care should always be taken with them and they should be handled with respect.

Here are some suggestions:

– Unaccompanied children should not be able to gain access to the vivarium room.
– Vivaria must be securely closed and in some cases locked.
– Vivaria and shelving should be solidly constructed and in no danger of shifting or collapsing.
– Electrical installations such as lighting and heating must meet the relevant standards.
– Beware of the irritating hairs of the New World tarantulas. These can cause severe inflammation, especially on the skin of children.
– Wash your hands immediately after handling tarantulas or their food.

The Taming, Training and "Obedience" of Tarantulas

To be able to keep tarantulas seriously and successfully, not only is a great deal of empathy needed but also an enormous amount of patience. Procedures with other vivarium animals may take only a relatively short time but with tarantulas they may take an entire decade. Tarantula keepers must, therefore, also have endurance.

Fig. 56. Despite all precautions, accidents can happen. This bite wound, inflicted by *Poecilotheria subfusca* (new taxonomy: *P. bara*) was painful for around 2 hours.

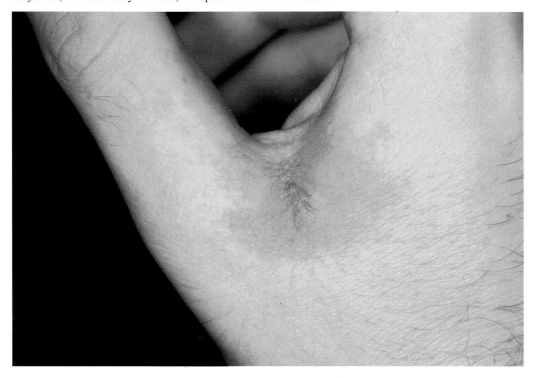

The desires for sensation or to earn money quickly should never be factors involved in wishing to keep tarantulas. Anyone simply wishing to be surrounded by a "multitude of exotics" has no real place in our fraternity.

In some of the more recent publications one can read that tarantulas can be easily tamed. That is nonsense! Like all other species of spiders, tarantulas are unable to communicate with humans in any way. They live in a sensory world which is im-

possible for us to understand. When confronted with a human, a tarantula will react in the same way as when confronted by any other threat—it will defend itself or try to escape. In this respect, individual genera and species have characteristic defense strategies. For example, if one picks up *Avicularia metallica* from the substrate, the animal holds on tight and turns its abdomen towards the intruding fingers. A layperson could assume the impression that the animal is friendly and wishes its abdomen to be "scratched." If, however, the finger which comes into contact with the abdomen is examined under a magnifying glass, it can be seen that the skin has been punctured by hundreds of abdominal hairs—a purely defensive measure.

Debilitated animals or those kept under unsuitable conditions will not show the full repertoire of their defensive behavior. This situation is often also misinterpreted as "tameness." If the misinterpretation of the tameness of tarantulas can be excused, then the assumptions of being obedient and trainable are simply comical. I would warn readers urgently and seriously to disregard the assumption that tarantulas can in any way form attachment or fondness for their keeper! The attempted "humanification" of pets with all its perverse results has already caused enough harm to many species of animals.

The toxicity of tarantulas has also been speculated about many times. There is enough scientific material available to prove without doubt that no species of tarantulas known to science to date can be really dangerous to humans. There are two reasons for this: tarantulas are very primitive spiders. While they have hardly changed during the course of evolution, other species of spiders have evolved to become the many species living today. In some species the venom glands have developed so strongly that they extend below the cephalothorax. The venom glands of tarantulas are in the chelicerae and are very small. Thus the amounts of venom are also small. Because of their great strength, tarantulas do not rely to any great extent on their toxicity. For millions of years they have relied on the strength of their chelicerae to capture their prey.

Nevertheless, because of the size of their fangs, a bite can be very painful. In some species the fangs may be up to 15 mm long. Because digestion takes place outside the body, the fangs are normally coated with large numbers of bacteria. Should these penetrate into the wound caused by the bite, they may cause severe inflammation. After a bite, the wound should, therefore, be immediately washed and disinfected.

Frequently Kept Tarantula Species

The species described here are only a small selection of spiders suitable for the vivarium. They are a representative cross-section of the species of tarantulas presently kept in captivity.

All details of the sizes of the spiders refer to the distance from the base of the chelicerae to the base of the spinneret, i.e., the actual body length. Unless otherwise stated, descriptions of color refer to newly molted animals.

Common names of individual species are frequently changed, sometimes without any significance. Therefore, anyone keeping spiders should at the outset learn the scientific name of each species. The most frequently used common names are also given.

The spiders included here may be identified by the photographs. Naturally there are many species of similar appearance. These may only be positively identified by closer examination of the sexual organs and other parts of the body. Scientific identification, however, is not the purpose of this book.

Details of vivaria sizes are all given in centimeters (length × width × height).

All scientific names given were valid at the time of printing, but the names of entire genera may be changed at any time.

American Species

Acanthoscurria gigantea
Chamberlin, 1939
Ecuadorian tarantula

Distribution: Ecuador
Maximum size: 11 cm
Description: *Acanthoscurria gigantea* is an extremely long-legged, ground-dwelling species of the subfamily Theraphosinae. The entire animal is a deep black. It is not especially hairy, but it does have some abdominal hair for defensive purposes. The long hairs on the abdomen may be a light red. Several months before it is due to molt its skin, *A. gigantea* assumes a dark rust red color giving the impression of a different species. This is a very aggressive urticating species.

Husbandry: Vivarium 30 × 20 × 20 cm or larger. Substrate is a 6–10 cm layer of leaf litter or peat/sand mixture. Use sparse furnishings with a halved flower pot for a hiding place. It may be planted with *Philodendron* or *Scindapsus*.

Because *A. gigantea* hails from montane regions of Ecuador, the temperature should not exceed 25 °C for long periods. My specimens have been kept for 6 years at a daytime temperature of 20–22 °C, dropping at night to 15–18 °C. It is essential that only undamaged specimens of this species are obtained.

Humidity should be 70–80%. The substrate should be constantly kept moist. *Acanthoscurria gigantea* has not yet been bred in captivity.

Behavior: *Acanthoscurria gigantea* exhibits very interesting defensive behavior. If molested it raises its body on all eight

Fig. 57. *Acanthoscurria gigantea* shortly before molting.

legs and will remain in this position for several minutes. If the disturbance continues it turns its abdomen toward the attacker and uses its hind legs to flick abdominal hair. Also while in this position the spider will eject a stream of excrement. Sometimes in the vivarium the spider will not be seen for several weeks, even at night. Be-

cause of its delicate nature and the special conditions for skin molting *A. gigantea* is not a suitable species for a beginner. Also *A. gigantea* is only rarely imported.

Aphonopelma chalcodes
Chamberlin, 1939
Mexican blond tarantula

Fig. 58. After molting, *Acanthoscurria gigantea* is again deep black.

Distribution: Arizona, United States
Maximum size: 9 cm
Description: Does not have the deep black coloring so typical of many tarantulas. Legs and carapace are light brown to beige while the abdomen is dark brown with longer light brown hairs. Typical of this genus is the strongly domed carapace. The chelicerae are particularly massive and the short, relatively stout legs indicate that this is a burrowing species. *Aphonopelma chalcodes* only rarely sheds urticating hairs. It is fairly aggressive and prone to bite.
Husbandry: Vivarium at least 20 × 30 × 20 cm. Substrate should be a 7–10 cm

Fig. 59. *Aphonopelma chalcodes.*

deep dry peat/sand mixture the greater proportion of which should be sand. Use flat pieces of bark for hiding places. Planting is almost impossible because of the burrowing habits of this species. One possibility is succulents without spines.

Temperatures should be 27–29 °C during the day with some parts of the vivarium cooler. At night the temperature may be reduced to 18–20 °C. Humidity is 60–70%. Illumination should preferably be from a fluorescent light. It is vital in the dry vivarium that fresh water is always available since *A. chalcodes* drinks a great deal.

Behavior: *Aphonopelma chalcodes* is an aggressive species which will not hesitate to bite if molested. In the vivarium it presents no problems. It eats large amounts causing the abdomen to become distended very quickly. It is then vital that the spider can not come into contact with sharp objects and must be handled very carefully to prevent it from being accidentally dropped. This species grows very slowly.

Breeding: Because *A. chalcodes* is only imported in very small numbers, one should attempt to obtain a viable breeding group. Imported adult males are very rare, and this species has not yet been bred in captivity.

Aphonopelma seemanni
Cambridge, 1897
Costa Rican zebra tarantula

Distribution: Panama, Costa Rica, Honduras to Guatemala
Maximum size: 8 cm
Description: It is very attractive, now frequently imported, very sturdily built and an aggressive species. The abdomen is black with long reddish hairs. The underside of the abdomen is a reddish orange and the spinnerets are also red. The carapace is a dark bluish gray. The legs are also bluish gray with long reddish hairs.

Fig. 60. (above) *Aphonopelma seemanni* female.
Fig. 61. (below) *Aphonopelma seemanni* male.

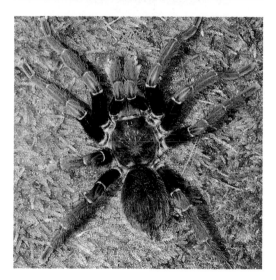

The pedipalps and the first pair of legs up to the patellae have parallel, longitudinal white stripes. The width of these stripes varies according to the population and locality. The stripes on the patellae of the rear legs are slightly diagonal. There are white rings at the joints of the legs. The tibia has two long white stripes. The upper third of the metatarsus has only one white stripe.

As molting approaches, the colors become paler. In some cases before molting they are a uniform brown without any stripes.

Sexual dimorphism is evident. The males are a deep black with a gold-colored carapace without stripes and with indistinct white rings at the joints.

Although *A. seemanni* has abdominal urticating hairs it is prone to defend itself with its chelicerae.

Husbandry: Undemanding regarding furnishing of the vivarium: $40 \times 30 \times 20$ cm. Daytime temperature should be 25–27 °C, dropping at night to 23 °C. Humidity should be ca. 70–80%. A deep substrate of compact soil corresponds to the natural habitat of this burrow-dwelling spider. In Costa Rica some populations have spread to cultivated land. There they prefer the very closely cut grassy areas and can even be found in sheep pastures. These dry meadows are usually on slopes and subject to constant sunshine. The population density is sometimes very high (1 to 3 spiders per 2 square meters). During the day this species hides in burrows which it excavates itself. The entrances are easily recognized. At night they sit at the burrow entrance in wait of prey, which in the wild is usually grasshoppers. It's a voracious feeder.

Breeding: The successful breeding of this very attractive species is extremely difficult. They are very nervous and are always ready to attack one another in their natural surroundings. Although my males will regularly spin sperm webs, they frequently grasp the larger females without copulation ever taking place.

Remarks: Be careful when handling these agile creatures because they often bite without warning. Once they become accustomed to their vivarium they make very amenable captives. This species is recommended for more experienced keepers. The main challenge is to achieve regular breeding. As is the case with all colorful and interestingly marked creatures, there is always the danger of over collecting, which can affect populations for a long time. Heavily decimated populations may take 15–20 years to recover!

Avicularia metallica Ausserer, 1875
Whitetoe tarantula

Distribution: Central America to Ecuador
Maximum size: 8 cm
Description: *Avicularia metallica* is a slender, medium-sized species which is recognized as a climbing, tree-dwelling species by the strong adhesive pads on the tarsus and metatarsus. The pink to light red

Fig. 62. According to geographic locality, the coloring of *Aphonopelma seemanni* can vary considerably.

Fig. 63. *Avicularia metallica.*

ends of the tarsi are plainly visible when the animal is moving. The ground color is a deep black, with some of the longer hairs having tips which are gray to white. Newly molted spiders are a shining metallic blue-black (hence the scientific name); moreover as a result of light refraction the clinging pads on the legs show all the colors of the rainbow.

Husbandry: Vivarium higher than it is long (20 × 20 × 30). Several branches or pieces of bark for climbing should be attached to the side and rear walls using an acetate-based silicone sealer.

Vines and branches from fruit trees are suitable. The vivarium may be planted with *Ficus repens* and *Scindapsus*. For the substrate use normal potting soil.

Ventilation should be reduced so that an atmospheric humidity of 70–80% is

Fig. 64. Until around the fifth molt *Avicularia metallica* is still very attractive.

Fig. 65. Until around the fifth molt *Avicularia metallica* is still very attractive.

achieved. Temperature during the daytime is 25–28 °C, the hottest part at 30 °C and nights at 20–25 °C. During the day, *A. metallica* enjoys sitting below the light and heat sources and often spins its web here, thus creating a home with central heating.

Breeding: *Avicularia metallica,* in my opinion, is the only tarantula species which may be considered as "social." A prerequisite here is that only sexually mature pairs are chosen, and all spiders should be well fed before being placed together. Such a pair will then live harmoniously together in a vivarium for around 6 months. During this period several copulations will take place. After around 10 to 12 months the male is usually too old for breeding and legs and palipalps tend to weaken, whereby he is unable to give the mating signals typical of this species. Frequently an older male will be found between the chelicerae of a female as the remains of a meal.

If a male is to copulate with several females, the procedure in the general section on breeding should be followed. Females ready to mate will take an active part in the courtship and mating displays during which she will approach the male and offer herself with foot-thumping signals. The actual copulation takes place without the female being treated aggressively.

Avicularia metallica is regularly bred in captivity. Six to ten weeks after copulation the female produces an eggsac inside its home web. This eggsac contains around 200 eggs. At an incubation temperature of 27 °C the young spiderlings hatch after around 9 weeks. Rearing the spiderlings presents no problems. After the eighth molt, male *A. metallica* are sexually mature.

Remarks: *Avicularia metallica* is a wonderful and interesting species. Good husbandry is rewarded by long life and lively behavior. After a short time in the vivarium it builds a large burrow from which it will often emerge during the daytime. Molting, feeding and oviposition take place in the burrow.

Avicularia metallica is one of the least aggressive of all tarantula species and may be handled at any time without danger. Its only defensive behavior is that it turns its hindquarters towards its "aggressor." On contact the minute abdominal hairs break off and may penetrate human skin.

Avicularia versicolor Wakkenaer, 1873
Antilles pinktoe tarantula

Distribution: Martinique
Maximum length: 6 cm
Description: A wonderful tree-dwelling spider of the subfamily Avicularinae. Its appearance is similar to that of *A. metallica*. The color of adults is a deep black without the red tarsus ends of *A. metallica*. Long pinkish red hairs cover the entire body. The young of this species are particularly beautiful. Up to the fifth or sixth molt they are a vivid blue color. This is a species which climbs and moves very quickly.
Husbandry: The size, furnishings and temperature of the vivarium are the same as for *A. metallica*. So that the animals may be more easily observed, only a small number of hiding places should be provided. Unfortunately, *A. versicolor* is rarely imported and has, therefore, not yet been bred in captivity in Germany. *Avicularia versicolor* is a hardy and enjoyable species suitable for a beginner.

Fig. 66. A young *Avicularia versicolor*.

Brachypelma albopilosa Valerio, 1980
Curlyhair tarantula

Distribution: Honduras to Panama
Maximum size: 8 cm
Description: Like all other *Brachypelma* species, *Brachypelma albopilosa* has a velvet-black ground coloring. The densely growing hairs are light brown, ending in a slightly curled tip giving this spider a very shaggy appearance. This is especially true of a newly molted animal. This is a species with urticating hairs.
Husbandry: Vivarium at least 20 × 30 × 20 cm. The substrate of dirt or potting soil should be around 5 cm deep and constantly kept slightly moist. The vivarium may be planted with *Scindapsus* or *Philo-*

Fig. 67. Unfortunately, with increasing age, the coloring of *Avicularia versicolor* becomes paler. The brownish ground color is replaced by an equally pleasing pink.

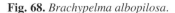

Fig. 68. *Brachypelma albopilosa.*

dendron scandens. Lighting preferably should be from a fluorescent lamp. *Brachypelma albopilosa* excavates a shallow burrow in loose earth. Temperature during the day should be 25–27 °C and not below 18 °C at night. Humidity should be 70–85%.

Breeding: Because all members of this genus are listed in CITES (Appendix II), captive breeding of these species is very

important. The blanket protection of entire genera is not necessarily justified, since some of the species may be very abundant in the wild. Also, exportation of new, undescribed species becomes impossible for the private collector. This also hinders those with scientific interests.

When breeding *B. albopilosa* it is best to wait until an adult female has molted. Two to four weeks after this molt the pair should be placed together for copulation. With un-bred females copulation presents no prob-lems. The female which at first is some-what uncooperative will soon assume the mating position. Six to ten weeks after mating the female digs a spacious burrow to lay her eggs in. The eggsac may contain up to 500 eggs. The spiderlings hatch after around 5 weeks at an incubation tempera-ture of 25 °C. After the initial molt the young should be housed separately and fed on *Drosophila* and later on houseflies. These spiders grow very quickly and may become sexually mature in 2 to 3 years.

Remarks: *Brachypelma albopilosa* is one of the most suitable tarantulas for the be-ginner. Its attractive appearance makes it interesting not only for the amateur but also for the expert. There is hardly a spider en-thusiast who does not have this specimen in his collection. It should be mentioned once again that if possible only animals which have been bred in captivity should be ob-tained. It is only in this way that the mass import of these creatures will cease.

Brachypelma auratum
(see *Brachypelma* sp.)

Brachypelma emilia White, 1856
Mexican redleg tarantula

Distribution: Costa Rica to Mexico
Maximum size: 7 cm

Description: *Brachypelma emilia, B. smithi* and *Megaphobema mesomelas* are at the top of the list of all spider enthusi-asts. All are extremely attractive. From the coxa to the patella the color is the black typical of all *Brachypelma* species. Tibia and metatarsus are vivid orange and the tarsus is black.

The carapace is also orange while the cephalic region is black so that as a black triangle it is in high contrast to the remain-der of the cephalothorax. The abdominal hairs are black interspersed with orange hairs. This is a species with urticating hairs.

Husbandry: Vivarium is 30 × 20 × 20 cm or larger. Substrate is a 5–10 cm deep layer of soil. As is the case with *B. smithi,* it is important for molting that this species is provided with a dry shelter of wood or bark.

Humidity is around 70%. Daytime tem-perature is 25–27 °C and not falling below 20 °C at night. Planting is not recom-mended because *B. emilia* is a burrowing species. Lighting should be preferably from a Gro-Lux fluorescent lamp.

Breeding: If sexually mature animals are available breeding should be attempted. Six to eight weeks after mating the female begins to dig in the vivarium. Inside a dense web she then produces a spherical eggsac. The number of eggs depends upon the size and species of the female, but is between 200 and 900!

Fig. 69. *Brachypelma emilia.*

Fig. 70. *Brachypelma mesomelas* (new taxonomy: *Megaphobema mesomelas*).

During the incubation of the eggsac the temperature should be kept constant at around 25 °C. The young hatch at around 10 weeks. After the initial molt they will begin to feed on *Drosophila*. After hatching the young measure around 5 mm and will grow very slowly Since *B. smithi* has recently become a protected species, *B. emilia* is now more frequently imported placing great pressure on the populations in Mexico. If this exploitation continues it will be no great surprise if this species is also included in Section II of the CITES. *Brachypelma emilia* is only suitable for experts who know how to care for *Brachypelma* species and are seriously attempting to breed these spiders.

Brachypelma mesomelas
Cambridge, 1897
New taxonomy: *Megaphobema mesomelas*
Costa Rican redleg tarantula

Distribution: Monte Verde region of Costa Rica
Maximum size: 6 cm
Description: A small to medium-sized *Megaphobema* species with very short hair giving it a very slender appearance. Only newly molted animals have complete abdominal hair. This is cast off at the slightest disturbance.

The particularly noticeable elongated carapace is black, as is the abdomen. Coxa to femur are also black. Patella, tibia and metatarsus are a deep orange color which gradually decreases in intensity. The tarsus is black.

This species is very calm and never aggressive. It is a rarely imported spider with urticating hairs.
Husbandry: A very moist vivarium with several hiding places, around 20 × 20 × 15 cm. The vivarium should be planted with Java moss and *Ficus repens*. The substrate should be a 5 cm deep layer of leaf

litter, partially rotted. Humidity should be at least 70%. Temperatures of 23–25 °C are adequate both day and night. Do not give food which is too large. Adult crickets are quite adequate.

Breeding: Nothing yet is known about the breeding of this species in nature. This is in all probability because no sexually mature animals are imported or at least the males are not mature. Moreover the care of *Megaphobema mesomelas* in the vivarium always presents some problems.

Because of the somewhat problematical husbandry of this very attractive species and the high prices which are charged for them, these species are not suitable for beginners.

Brachypelma smithi Cambridge, 1897
Mexican redknee tarantula

Distribution: Mexico
Maximum size: 8 cm
Description: *Brachypelma smithi* is a typical ground-dwelling species. Typical of the genus is the compact sturdy habitus and the velvety-black ground color. All *Brachypelma* species have urticating hair. The irritating hairs of *B. smithi* can cause swelling of the mucous membranes, bouts of coughing and weeks of itchy irritation. Therefore, these animals should be handled carefully, especially by children.

As well as the velvety-black coloring *B. smithi* has many long hairs over the entire body (with the exception of the carapace). These hairs are light brown to orange in color. The tarsus and metatarsus have a light brown band on the distal portion, as does the patella which has a deep orange spot on the upper side. The carapace is black and has light brown peripheral hairs.

Husbandry: In contrast to the opinion of many tarantula enthusiasts, *B. smithi* is not an easy species to keep. A badly maintained individual will sometimes "survive" for up to 3 years but will not feed and will eventually die. The disappointed keeper will usually never blame himself and will normally seek an immediate replacement. For this reason, *B. smithi* was for some time the most frequently purchased of all tarantula species.

In accordance with the size which *B. smithi* can reach, the vivarium should have a minimum ground area of 30 × 20 cm. The substrate should be a 5 cm deep layer of potting soil which should be kept slightly moist. Humidity should be between 70 and 80%. Daytime temperature stays around 27 °C dropping at night to not below 19 °C.

During molting *B. smithi* requires a flat or bowl-shaped piece of bark or cork bark which should be placed in the vivarium when it is initially furnished.

Fig. 71. *Brachypelma smithi.*

Breeding: The courtship and mating behavior of *B. smithi* has already been described in the section "Courtship and Mating." Breeding is not easy. The greatest difficulty is in obtaining males and ensuring that both animals are in breeding condition at the same time.

Four to six weeks after copulation the female produces an eggsac in a shelter which it excavates itself. This can contain up to 1000 eggs. Such a large number of eggs is not, however, the rule. At an incubation temperature of 25 °C the young hatch after 8 to 11 weeks. The very small spiderlings (ca. 0.5 mm) molt after 2 to 3 weeks and will then begin feeding on *Drosophila*.

Remarks: Because it is now contained in Appendix II of the CITES Agreement, this spider has become very rare in zoological dealers' shops. It would therefore appear reasonable that all spiders remaining in captivity should be gathered together to form the nucleus of a breeding group. Only in this way will this beautiful species remain available to us.

Brachypelma **sp.**
New taxonomy: *Brachypelma auratum* Schmidt, 1992
Mexican flameknee tarantula

Distribution: Mexico
Maximum size: 8 cm

Description: For a long time this species was considered to be only a color variant of *B. smithi*. However, this is not the case because the behavior of this species is totally different from that of *B. smithi*. On the one hand, when molested it reacts rather differently than *B. smithi* does and on the other hand it is capable of producing audible stridulation sounds which indicate that the construction of its body is different from that of *B. smithi*.

Brachypelma auratum is built more slenderly than *B. smithi*. The ground color is a deep black. The patella and pedipalp have a very sharply defined red spot on the dorsal surface. As opposed to *B. smithi* this presents a wonderful contrast to the black on the underside of the patella. In addition, at the end of each patella, tibia and metatarsus there is a white or orange-colored ring. *Brachypelma auratum* is unfortunately only rarely available commercially. This is a nonaggressive species with urticating hairs.

Husbandry: This species should be kept in the same way as *Brachypelma smithi* but with the humidity somewhat higher. The vivarium should be larger than $30 \times 20 \times 20$ cm because this species frequently wanders around. Nothing is known about captive breeding. In my collection a newly imported, wild-caught female built an eggsac containing around 600 eggs which unfortunately did not develop.

Fig. 72. *Brachypelma* sp. (new taxonomy: *B. auratum*).

Brachypelma vagans (Ausserer, 1875)
Mexican redrump tarantula

Distribution: Guatemala, Honduras
Maximum size: 8 cm
Description: Ground color velvety-black.
The abdominal hairs are also deep black
with longer interspersed vivid red hairs.
The border of the carapace is white to orange. Spiders which are about to molt appear brown. This is a very calm spider with
urticating hairs.
Husbandry: Vivarium 30 × 20 × 20 cm
or larger. Substrate should be a 7 cm deep

Fig. 73. *Brachypelma vagans.*

layer of soil/sand mixture or ordinary potting soil. Room temperature is quite adequate for this species, but should not, however, be below 17 °C. A suitable daytime
temperature is 25 °C, reduced to 20–22 °C
at night. Humidity is 60–70%.

A vivarium may be planted if it is large
enough, and then illuminated by a fluorescent lamp.

Breeding: *Brachypelma vagans* has been
bred several times in captivity. Only 4
weeks after mating the female produces an
eggsac which contains around 300 eggs.
With high humidity (about 75%) the

greater part of the clutch will spoil. The young hatch in 9 weeks and after a further 14 days will take the first food. Rearing the young presents no problems. A humidity of 70–80% and an average temperature of 26 °C allow the young to grow very quickly.

Remarks: In general, imports of *Brachypelma vagans* are only available every 2 to 4 years, so males are only available at these times. If breeding is intended, not only adults but also smaller individuals should be obtained. Captive bred young are frequently available. *Brachypelma vagans* is easy to keep and gives a great deal of pleasure to an experienced keeper.

Cyclosternum fasciatum
(see *Metriopelma zebrata*)

Dugesiella (syn. *Aphonopelma*) *anax*
Chamberlin, 1939
Texas tan tarantula

Distribution: Texas, United States
Maximum size: 5 cm
Description: A compact burrowing species with strong chelicerae and ground color of black or brown. The carapace is a bronze color with a metallic sheen. The legs have long bronze-colored hairs. The abdomen is black with longer bronze-colored hairs. In the young these hairs are red. It is a mildly aggressive spider with urticating hairs.
Husbandry: The vivarium should be somewhat larger than 30 × 20 × 20 cm, and substrate should be a 7–8 cm deep layer of soil/sand mixture. Various cork bark tubes and pieces should be provided as hiding places. It is advisable to plant the vivarium with *Scindapsus*. Daytime temperature should be 20–23 °C, not falling below 15 °C at night.

Dugesiella has been bred several times in captivity. At present I have 40 young specimens. This is a slow-growing species which is nevertheless a worthwhile captive because of its hardiness and interesting behavior and is, therefore, recommended for beginners. Hopefully in the future wild-caught animals will no longer need to be imported.

Ephebopus murinus Karsch, 1880
Skeleton tarantula

Distribution: French Guiana
Maximum size: 5 cm
Description: Like the closely related *Paraphysa pulcherrimaklaasi*, *E. murinus* has well-developed tarsal and metatarsal adhesive pads. The ground color is black and the carapace is gray-brown. Because of the longitudinal white stripes on the patella and tibia this species is frequently confused with *Aphonopelma seemanni*. On the ground *Ephebopus murinus* excavates deep tunnels, the entrance to which is broadened by a wide silken funnel, where

E. murinus sits awaiting prey. When molested this spider retreats rapidly into its burrow. It is a somewhat aggressive species.

Husbandry: Vivarium 20 × 30 × 20 cm or larger with a 5–10 cm deep layer of soil/sand mixture as substrate. A hiding place of a cork bark tube is acceptable. Humidity should be 60–70%. Temperature throughout the day and night should be 26–28 °C. *Ephebopus murinus* is easy to keep and is a suitable species for the beginner. Unfortunately, however, it is only rarely available making it imperative that captive breeding be attempted.

Ephebopus violaceus Mello-Leitao, 1930
New taxonomy: *Paraphysa pulcherrimaklaasi* Schmidt, 1992
No common name

Distribution: Ecuador, up to an altitude of 500 m
Maximum size: 6 cm
Description: *Paraphysa pulcherrimaklaasi* is a medium-sized, slenderly built tarantula belonging to the subfamily Eumenophorinae from the tropical rain forest regions of Ecuador. Well-developed adhesive pads allow this spider to climb trees

Fig. 76. *Ephobopus violaceus* (new taxonomy: *Paraphysa pulcherrimaklaasi*).

and live among the bromeliads growing there. The gold-colored carapace has a metallic sheen under certain lighting conditions. The abdomen is black with very fine and dense hairs which may also have a metallic sheen. The proximal end of the femur is dark blue, the rest of the limb brown with a white-striped pattern. It is a very peaceful species which only rarely uses its abdominal hair for defensive purposes.

Husbandry: A vivarium of $20 \times 30 \times 50$ cm should be furnished as a tropical arboreal habitat. Humidity should be up to 85%. Temperatures should be between 25 and 27 °C both day and night. Extensive planting will offer further climbing possi-

bilities; natural plants to use include bromeliads. The substrate should be a 5 cm deep layer of potting soil. Hiding places in the form of cork bark should be provided.
Breeding: Because of a shortage of sexually mature animals this species has not yet been bred in captivity. It would be wonderful if only one large shipment of these creatures could be imported in the near future. This species is easy to keep and because of its climbing activities will give great pleasure to its keeper.

Grammostola pulchripes Simon, 1891
No common name

Distribution: Argentina
Maximum size: 11 cm
Description: *Grammostola pulchripes* is one of the largest tarantulas in the world. It is not very conspicuous regarding color and pattern but its size alone (a leg span of up to 28 cm) makes it one of the most sought after spiders. The ground color is chocolate brown. Over the entire body, older specimens have a greenish sheen and long reddish-brown hairs, especially on the abdomen. The abdominal irritating hairs are very fine and arranged as a shimmering silver patch. This is a nonaggressive spider with urticating hairs.
Husbandry: Vivarium at least 60 × 40 × 40 cm. The substrate should be a layer of bark mulch or potting soil covered by a layer of leaf litter. A large hiding place

Fig. 77. *Grammostola pulchripes.*

should also be provided, such as a nesting box for birds. The temperature during the day should be 20–22 °C and at night should not fall below 18 °C. Humidity should be around 65%. It is a very easily-kept species. If the vivarium is allowed to dry out occasionally this will be tolerated by the spiders for several weeks. The females may reach an almost biblical age of up to 25 years.
Breeding: This species is not yet bred regularly in captivity. At present I am rearing 20 spiderlings which were born from an imported female. During air transport from Brazil the female constructed an eggsac from which the young emerged after only 3 weeks. With good fortune perhaps the males will become sexually mature at the same time as the females. If this were to be the case it would then be possible to breed this long-lived species regularly.

Fig. 78. *Grammostola pulchripes.*

Grammostola spatulata
(see *Phrixotrichus roseus*)

Lasiodora klugi Koch, 1842
No common name

Distribution: Brazil
Maximum size: 9 cm
Description: The large species of the genus *Lasiodora* are the pride and joy of any collection of spiders. They do not have any special markings. It is purely their size

and dense, long hairs which make them so sought after. *Lasiodora klugi* is a compact ground-dwelling species which also climbs well. Legs and cephalothorax are brown, turning to light brown before molting. The abdomen is black with long flame-red hairs.

The hairs on *Lasiodora klugi* give it a very "unkept" appearance.

In comparison to the equally large Grammostolinae, *Lasiodora* species are usually very aggressive. *Lasiodora* species have a great ability to cast off their urticating hairs.

Husbandry: Vivarium at least 40 × 30 × 30 cm. Bark pieces should be fastened to the rear and side walls of the vivarium because *Lasiodora* frequently climbs. The vivarium may be planted with *Philodendron scandens*. Temperature during the day should be 22–26 °C, falling to 20 °C at night.

Humidity should be around 70%. A spacious hiding place should be provided. The substrate should be well-compacted potting soil covered with leaf litter.

Breeding: Because of a shortage of sexually mature animals, breeding is only occasionally achieved. My specimens were obtained as spiderlings in 1979, but unfortunately all proved to be female thus making breeding impossible. At an average temperature of 22 °C the spiderlings grew very slowly and it is only now that they are

Fig. 79. *Lasiodora klugi.*

sexually mature. I would, therefore, suggest that for rearing this species somewhat higher temperatures are required.

Remarks: *Lasiodora klugi* is an easily kept species which unfortunately is only rarely available. To breed this species in captivity it will be necessary to import some new animals from Brazil.

Megaphobema mesomelas **(see *Brachypelma mesomelas*)**

Metriopelma **(syn. *Crypsidromus*)** *colorata* Valerio, 1982
No common name

Distribution: Brazil
Maximum size: 3 cm

Fig. 80. *Metriopelma colorata.*

Description: A small spider, like many *Metriopelma* species, that has very conspicuous markings. Grayish-brown legs. The cephalic part of the cephalothorax is rusty-red; the rest of the cephalothorax is black. At the posterior of the thorax the radial stripes are red and contrast strongly with the black background. The ground color of the abdomen is black. On the upper third of the abdomen there is a circular red blotch. The sides of the abdomen have four wide blotches which gradually become smaller toward the spinnerets. This is a species with urticating hairs.

This spider, in my opinion, is the most attractive of all *Metriopelma* species but unfortunately, it is only rarely imported. Although some years ago animals were regularly imported from Brazil, now they are strictly protected. Therefore it is only possible to obtain these spiders privately from other spider enthusiasts. For this reason it is essential that breeding is attempted if we want to continue to have these creatures available. That this should not be too difficult is proven by the fact that the closely related species *Cyclosternum fasciatum* and *M. drymusetes,* which have been bred in captivity, are regularly available both commercially and privately.

The size of the vivarium is unimportant for this spider but it must be kept somewhat warmer than the other two related species. It should be kept at 26–27 °C. It should not be fed on large insects such as field or house crickets because it only reaches a maximum body length of 3 cm. Houseflies, however, are ideally suited.

The nomenclature of the genera *Crypsidromus* and *Metriopelma* is at present in the process of being changed. For that reason both names have been given here.

Fig. 81. *Metriopelma drymusetes.*

Metriopelma (syn. *Crypsidromus*) *drymusetes* Valerio, 1982
Wasp tarantula

Distribution: Costa Rica
Maximum size: 3.5 cm
Description: *Metriopelma drymusetes* is very similar in appearance to the closely related *Cyclosternum fasciatum*. The main difference is in the color of the legs. *Cyclosternum fasciatum zebratus* has black legs; those of *M. drymusetes* are grayish-blue after molting. A second differentiating characteristic is the presence of very large tibial spurs in the males, while in *C. fasciatum* they are very small or absent. This species has urticating hairs.
Husbandry: As with *C. fasciatum* a vivar-ium temperature of 25 °C is quite adequate for *M. drymusetes*. The vivarium furnishings may also be the same.

Some enthusiasts who have specialized in these small tarantula species have had great success with these wonderful spiders by keeping them in very small vivaria. Because of their small size they must only be given small prey insects. Houseflies are ideal. Half-grown crickets may also be given provided the jumping legs have been removed. Small mealworms may also be added to the menu. A small vivarium for *Metriopelma* species can be especially attractive if it is furnished with various mosses and ferns. These plants improve the microclimate and increase the atmospheric humidity considerably.

Fig. 82. *Metriopelma drymusetes.*

***Metriopelma* (syn. *Crypsidromus*) *zebrata* Banks, 1909**
New taxonomy: *Cyclosternum fasciatum* Valerio
Costa Rican tigerrump tarantula

Distribution: Central America
Maximum size: 4 cm
Description: A small but very attractive species of the subfamily Ischnocolinae. Legs almost black. Cephalothorax a reddish-brown with a metallic sheen. The ground color of the abdomen is black with a reddish-brown pattern of seven stripes on each side. This is the most frequently imported Ischnocoline species. It is a quick moving, urticating spider which also climbs well.

Fig. 83. *Metriopelma zebrata* male (new taxonomy: *Cyclosternum fasciatum*).

Husbandry: A small or medium-sized vivarium around 15 × 20 × 20 cm, higher than it is long. *Cyclosternum fasciatum* likes to sit in warm places and is not disturbed by bright lights. The daytime temperature should be 24–26 °C and at night it should not drop below 20 °C. The substrate should be a 2–5 cm deep layer of soil upon which a layer of bark should be placed as hiding places. Humidity should be 75–90%. Lighting from a fluorescent lamp is desirable.

Breeding: While serious attempts to breed *C. fasciatum* should be made, the main prerequisite for this is mature adults. Because *C. fasciatum* is only rarely imported it is best to obtain captive-bred young which are bred every 1 to 2 years. The spiderlings

Fig. 84. A young *Metriopelma zebrata* (new taxonomy: *Cyclosternum fasciatum*).

grow very slowly. Unfortunately the maximum life expectancy of *C. fasciatum* is only 3–4 years, but for a spider that is indeed a ripe old age. This species is easy to breed although the animals are relatively aggressive toward their mates. The spiderlings are extremely small (total length 2.5 mm). Their first food should be minute insects such as springtails or *Drosophila melanogaster*.

Paraphysa pulcherrimaklaasi (see *Ephebopus violaceus*)

Phormictopus cancerides (Latreille, 1806)
Haitian brown tarantula

Distribution: Haiti, islands of the West Indies
Maximum size: 7 cm
Description: A large, slenderly built species. The metatarsi of the last pair of legs are twice as long as those of the other legs. Rear legs measuring 9 cm are not uncommon. Usually fully grown males have long, thin rear legs. The metatarsus and tarsus have wide adhesive pads. In older animals shortly before molting the ground color is a uniform russet-red. Young animals are a reddish-brown. Newly molted animals are darker (chocolate-brown) with a wonderful metallic-red sheen to the cephalothorax. Adult males also have a metallic-red femur. Although without any pattern worth mentioning, nevertheless its a spider that is very attractive because of its dense hair. Care should be taken when handling this somewhat aggressive species. It is a spider with urticating hairs that does not make any stridulation noises.
Husbandry: A semi-arid rocky vivarium of at least 20 × 30 × 20 cm, preferably 40 × 30 × 20 cm. The substrate should be a 3–5 cm deep layer of soil covered with leaf litter which is slightly moist. This is a confirmed ground dweller that rarely digs. A spacious hiding place in the form of cork bark or a wood nesting box as used for birds is acceptable. These spiders drink frequently and should be fed regularly to ensure proper growth. Temperature should be 22–28 °C during the day and not below 15 °C at night. The temperature drop at night is desirable. Humidity should be 70% during the day, rising to 85% at night. The vivarium should be well-ventilated and may be planted with grasses and *Philodendron scandens*. This species should be given large prey insects such as locusts and deaths head beetles.
Breeding: I first obtained this species in 1979, as 5 mm spiderlings from the Cologne Zoo. At a temperature of 27 °C they may be reared without difficulty. Males may become sexually mature after only a year, however, females may require up to 3 years. This species is not difficult to breed. Well fed females will lay eggs around 4 weeks after copulation. At a temperature of around 27 °C the young emerge from the eggsac after a further 4 weeks. When they reach a size of 6 mm the spiderlings will be able to eat houseflies after which they will grow very quickly. Until around the fifth molt the spiderlings are a beautiful blue-black color. This spider is especially suitable for beginners. Small to medium-sized specimens adapt to life in the vivarium more quickly.

Phrixotrichus roseus Pocock, 1903
New taxonomy: *Grammostola spatulata* Cambridge, 1897
Chilean rose tarantula

Distribution: Chile
Maximum size: 7 cm

Fig. 85. *Phormictopus cancerides.*

Description: At the present time *Grammostola spatulata* is one of the most frequently imported of all tarantula species. The correct identification of these creatures, however, is difficult since in the course of time they have been given a multitude of generic and species names. One reason for this is the highly variable coloration ranging from dark brown through beige to an intense orange-red according to their geographic origin.

Common to all animals is a metallic-red sheen on the carapace. From the pedicel a black band extends to the first third of the abdomen. In some specimens, however, this black band may be absent. Orange-colored specimens do not lose their color-

Fig. 86. A young *Phormictopus cancerides.*

ing before molting. The abdominal urticating hairs are only rarely used for defensive purposes.

Husbandry: Vivarium at least 30 × 20 × 20 cm. If the substrate is too moist, the tarsus may easily become moldy. For this reason the substrate of peat moss or potting soil should be covered by a 5–6 cm thick layer of finely ground tree bark. Suitable hiding places are arch-shaped pieces of bark glued together or a halved flower pot. Temperature during the day should be 25–28 °C to 22 °C at night. Because this spider will only make a very poor recovery from loss of weight it must be fed regularly.

Breeding: *Grammostola spatulata* is frequently bred in captivity. Despite a

Fig. 87. *Psalmopoeus cambridgei*, male.

very short development period of 3½ weeks at 27 °C the spiderlings grow very slowly even when being very well maintained. The newly hatched spiderlings are very small and thus are only able to eat small insects such as *Drosophila*.

I obtained some spiderlings in 1982. At normal room temperature the females were only sexually mature in 1988. The males were fully grown around a year earlier and then began to die off.

If the growth of males is artificially slowed, sexually mature partners may eventually be obtained from their siblings. Copulation is not exactly peaceful. If the female becomes too aggressive the pair must be separated.

Remarks: A somewhat sensitive species, *G. spatulata* is nevertheless also suitable for a beginner. Because this species is regularly bred in captivity it is relatively easy to obtain and the supply of captive-bred specimens seems assured.

Fig. 88. *Psalmopoeus cambridgei*. The front legs of males are very hairy.

Fig. 89. A newly molted *Psalmopoeus cambridgei*.

wide because of the sideways-growth of the hairs. Tarsus and metatarsus have a deep orange stripe, and the carapace is olive green. The ground color of the entire spider is beige. The abdomen has a dark triangular marking. When resting, this spider will often stretch out completely with the first pair of legs and the pedipalps lying parallel to the longitudinal axis of the body. This is an especially agile tree-dwelling tarantula.

Husbandry: A tall vivarium for tree-dwelling species, at least 20 × 30 × 50 cm. Several climbing branches. Lighting and heating from fluorescent lamps. The potting soil substrate should constantly be kept moist. The temperature should be 25–27 °C, localized in places to 30 °C during the day. At night the temperature should not fall below 20 °C. Humidity should be 75–80%. *Psalmopoeus cambridgei* spins large residential webs in the

Psalmopoeus cambridgei Pocock, 1895
Trinidad chevron tarantula

Distribution: Trinidad
Maximum size: 8 cm
Description: Next to *Avicularia metallica* one of the most important tree-dwelling species of the subfamily Avicularinae. Very long legs which appear extremely

Fig. 90. *Psalmopoeus cambridgei.*

Fig. 91. *Psalmopoeus reduncus.*

The young will immediately eat small houseflies. Even at an age of only 2 months they have a leg span of 4 cm.

Remarks: This tarantula should form the nucleus of any collection of giant spiders. Its magnificent size and attractive appearance make it an impressive addition to any collection.

Psalmopoeus reduncus Karsch, 1880
Costa Rican orangemouth tarantula

Distribution: Costa Rica
Maximum size: 6 cm
Description: Smaller and more compactly built than *P. cambridgei.* Ground color dark brown to almost black. The cephalothorax is somewhat lighter. Legs are relatively thick with strong adhesive pads. Adult males are very thickly haired making them look much larger than the females. They have no urticating hairs on the abdomen, are easily irritated and very quick.

Husbandry: Vivarium 20 × 30 × 20 cm. The substrate should be a 5 cm deep layer of soil or sand/soil mixture. Pieces of flat bark can be used as hiding places. In a short space of time *Psalmopoeus reduncus* will construct the underground burrow in which it lives. The excavated substrate is piled by the entrance and the entire surface covered with a very dense web. A temperature of 22–25 °C is sufficient both day and night. Humidity should be around 70%.

upper reaches of the vivarium. To service these vivaria properly, access should be from the side, so that the residential web is not disturbed causing the spiders to spring from the vivarium.

If *P. cambridgei* is disturbed it will often drop to the ground and run quickly to the nearest hiding place. This spider may jump a distance of up to 20 cm.

Breeding: This species is regularly bred in captivity. This is very important since *P. cambridgei* is now only very rarely imported and wild-caught animals are almost impossible to obtain. During copulation this species is often aggressive.

Under the same incubation conditions as those described for *Avicularia metallica,* the spiderlings hatch after around 8 weeks.

Fig. 92. *Pterinopelma saltator.*

Unfortunately only very few enthusiasts keep *Psalmopoeus reduncus* which is a great pity. On the basis of its hardiness and above all because it is easy to breed, this spider, like *A. metallica* should form the basis of any collection of giant spiders.

Pterinopelma saltator Pocock, 1903
No common name

Distribution: Argentina
Maximum size: 5 cm
Description: An attractive species that does not grow too large. Carapace dark gray with a cream-colored border. The pedipalps and first three pairs of legs have a black ground color with long light gray hairs giving the cephalothorax an overall gray appearance. The abdomen is a deep black. It is interesting to note that in contrast to the others the rear legs are always black but when placed alongside the hindquarters they blend in perfectly. It is a very peaceful spider with urticating hairs that is in no way aggressive.
Husbandry: A small vivarium around 15 × 20 × 20 cm. The substrate should be a layer of leaf litter only 2–3 cm deep. This should be kept very moist. Hiding places in the form of arched pieces of cork bark are acceptable. High humidity is up to 90%. Daytime temperatures should be 22–24 °C, falling to 19–20 °C at night. The vivarium should be planted with Java moss and small ferns. This easily kept species causes no problems and is recommended for any spider enthusiast. Unfortunately this species is not yet bred regularly in captivity.

Rhechostica sp.
Goldbacked tarantula

Distribution: Tucson, Arizona
Maximum size: 7 cm
Description: A wonderfully attractive but unfortunately rarely imported species. Legs are black and abdomen is black with long red hairs similar to *B. vagans*. The gold-colored cephalothorax is in brilliant contrast to the legs and abdomen. Males are usually smaller. The spider has urticating hairs.
Husbandry: A spacious vivarium which, because of the considerable size of the spider, must not be less than 40 cm in length. The substrate should be a 5 cm deep layer of peat mixed with coarse sand and should be kept almost dry. Cork bark or stacked flat rocks are usable as hiding places. Humidity should be 60–80%. Daytime temperature should be 22–25 °C, falling to at least 20 °C at night. Fresh water is necessary daily. This species appreciates the mild heat radiated from a fluorescent lamp.
Remarks: A very attractive and easily kept species particularly suitable for a beginner. Animals which were recently sent to me from Arizona proved to be exclusively male making breeding impossible in the near future. Because of their reluctance to bite and their peaceful temperament this is an excellent and interesting spider for any collection.

Fig. 93. Depending upon geographic locality, the coloring of *Phrixotrichus roseus* (new taxonomy: *Grammostola spatulata*) can vary considerably.

Fig. 94. (above) Depending upon geographic locality, the coloring of *Phrixotrichus roseus* (new taxonomy: *Grammostola spatulata*) can vary considerably.
Fig. 95. (below) *Rhechostica* sp., male.

For captive breeding to take place, mature animals of both sexes must first be obtained.

Sericopelma generala Valerio, 1980
No common name

Distribution: Costa Rica, e.g., along the Rio Generale
Maximum size: 8 cm
Description: A large, stout spider of the subfamily Theraphosinae. In appearance it is very similar to *Theraphosa blondi,* but it only has very short hairs on the legs and cephalothorax. The abdomen has long flame-red hairs. The ground color is uniform chocolate brown with long red hairs on the abdomen. Males of the species *S. generala* and *S. immensa* appear to be uniform black and have bright red abdomens. Newly molted females are also deep black with flame-red abdominal hairs. This spider is always ready to bite, but its size makes it a very attractive species.
Husbandry: Vivarium at least 40 × 30 × 30 cm. The substrate in the vivarium should be arranged in a steep slope. Cork or wooden tubes should be inserted horizontally into the substrate. These will serve as entrances into the residential hole which the spider will soon excavate.

The temperature should not be too high. During the day 20–23 °C is quite adequate, at night 20 °C will suffice. Humidity should be 65%. *Sericopelma generala* is a

Fig. 96. *Rhechostica* sp.

very greedy feeder and should be given large food insects.

Breeding: No one yet has succeeded in breeding this species. Hopefully new imports will allow this species to be bred in captivity in the near future. I have only kept this species for a short time and presently can not give exact information about its longevity. To date these spiders have been easy to care for.

Sphaerobothria hoffmanni Karsch, 1879
No common name

Distribution: Costa Rica
Maximum size: 5 cm

Fig. 97. (above) *Sericopelma generala.*
Fig. 98. (below) *Sericopelma generala,* male.

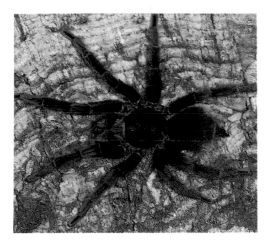

Description: A plainly colored and stoutly built tarantula from Central America. The cephalothorax of the females is dark olive-brown. The legs from the patellae to the tarsi are somewhat lighter. The abdomen ground color is black with long, light gray hairs. This species is unmistakable because of a button-like protuberance in a depression on the cephalothorax, similar to that in the African genus *Ceratogyrus.* Males are dark brown with a metallic bronze cephalothorax. The button-like protuberance of the males is considerably shorter.

Husbandry: In the wild this spider digs narrow tunnels several meters long, even bypassing rocks and tree roots. For this reason a long vivarium with a large floor space is necessary. The substrate should be a mixture of peat and sand (1:2). The height of the vivarium is unimportant. The temperature on the ground should be 20–22 °C while the air temperature may safely rise to 27 °C.

Remarks: In its natural habitat *Sphaerobothria hoffmanni* is quite common but when being caught this burrowing species suffers such great stress that it rarely survives. It is, however, easily kept in the vivarium and in theory breeding should be possible. In the vivarium this species is very peaceful, indeed even lethargic, and sometimes remains in the hiding place for several weeks. Well-fed animals are rarely seen. If they are not overfed they may be seen at dusk hunting for prey. Unfortunately, in 1986 I received only one adult pair of this species. Despite copulation taking place several times, the female did not produce an eggsac and molted in February 1987.

Fig. 99. *Sphaerobothria hoffmanni.*

Fig. 100. *Theraphosa blondi.*

During this time the male died. I must, therefore, obtain new animals in an effort to reproduce this species which is so interesting because of its curious appearance.

Theraphosa blondi Latreille, 1804
Goliath birdeater tarantula

Distribution: French Guiana, Venezuela
Maximum size: 12 cm
Description: *Theraphosa blondi* is one of

the largest and heaviest tarantulas on earth. Its coloration is not particularly striking, but it is distinguished by its very strong legs with their dense, long hairs. Specimens that are badly cared for or are just about to molt appear very bare and are a russet-red color. The ground color is rich black, but because of the long, light brown hairs the spider appears to be uniform dark brown. The abdominal hairs are rarely all present. This is because *Theraphosa*

Fig. 101. *Theraphosa blondi* should only be handled in exceptional circumstances.

blondi regularly lines its home and entrances with the hairs. This species is aggressive with urticating hairs.

Husbandry: Vivarium 60 × 30 × 40 cm. The substrate should be a peat moss or a mixture of peat and bark chippings at least 6–10 cm deep, covered by a layer of dry oak or beech leaves. A dark spacious hiding place formed from large pieces of bark should be provided.

Humidity should be between 85 and 98% with a daytime temperature of 25–27 °C, falling to 23 °C at night. It is very sensitive to standing water, which causes the tarsus to mold. For this reason condensation on the glass walls of the vivarium should be prevented by adequate ventilation. This species should be fed on large cockroaches and locusts. The abdomen may sometimes reach the size of a tennis ball.

Breeding: *Theraphosa blondi* has been bred several times in captivity. The female is at first somewhat aggressive, but if in breeding condition, will allow the male to mate with her for around 10 minutes. After mating the pair will separate without any further aggressive behavior. The males of *Theraphosa blondi* have no tibial spurs.

While the eggs are being incubated, *Theraphosa blondi* spins itself completely into its living quarters.

Depending upon the incubation temperature the young hatch after 8 to 10 weeks. After a further 14 days the young molt for the first time.

It is worth mentioning that after hatching the young already measure 15 mm! Even the hind quarters with the yolksac have the dimensions of a large pea. After only the third molt the leg span measures 5 cm. The rearing of the young is, however, problematic.

Remarks: *Theraphosa blondi* still presents considerable problems in the vivarium. One of the main reasons is that imported animals usually arrive damaged or in a very weakened condition. Another reason is the bad conditions under which they are kept at dealers' premises. It would simplify matters considerably if these conditions could be improved. The best spiders without doubt are those brought by private enthusiasts from the country of origin.

Fig. 102. *Ceratogyrus brachycephalus.*

African Species

Ceratogyrus brachycephalus
Hewitt, 1919
Greaterhorned tarantula

Distribution: South Africa, Transvaal
Maximum size: 4 cm
Description: A small, squat species that is somewhat more compact than *C. darlingi*. The ground color is beige or light brown and the cephalothorax is light brown. A thick black horn protudes ante-riorly from the thorax. I have not yet seen a male of this species. As in *C. darlingi* there is a yellowish-orange band in the genital area.
Husbandry: The vivarium may be some-what smaller than that described for *C. darlingi*. Light, temperature and humid-ity are the same as that for *C. darlingi*. *Ceratogyrus brachycephalus* prefers in-sects the size of medium field or adult house crickets. Large crickets are some-times able to fight off the spider. The

Fig. 103. *Ceratogyrus brachycephalus.*

spines on the jumping legs of adult crickets may also damage the abdomen of the spider.

Breeding: To date, this spider has not yet been bred regularly in captivity. From a wild-caught female I obtained an eggsac from which around 100 spiderlings hatched. The spiderlings would only eat the most minute food. The mortality rate, however, was around 90% and unfortunately only four of the young lived to adulthood.

Ceratogyrus darlingi Pocock, 1897
Horned tarantula

Distribution: South Africa, Transvaal
Maximum size: 7 cm
Description: Ground color slate gray but after molting also light brown. There is no distinct pattern on the cephalothorax or extremities. The abdomen is relatively small with a black central stripe on a brown background. Transverse stripes begin at the central stripe. Sternum and undersides of the legs are a deep rich black. The underside of the abdomen is also black with yellow or orange bands in the genital area.

All *Ceratogyrus* species have a horn protruding from a depression on the cephalothorax. The size of this horn and the direction in which it points varies from species to species. In this species it is quite short and points backwards. The function of this horn is not yet known.

Ceratogyrus darlingi is sexually dimorphic. This means that the external appearance of males is very different from females. The male is considerably smaller (maximum size 5 cm), has a darker color and has narrow white rings at the joints of the limbs.

Husbandry: For this species a vivarium of 20 × 20 × 20 cm is suitable. Because *Ceratogyrus* species spin a very dense web sometimes covering the entire vivarium they are only rarely visible. This makes it extremely difficult to monitor their

Fig. 104. *Ceratogyrus darlingi.*

progress. Therefore, it is essential that *Ceratogyrus* species (as well as *Pterinochilus* and *Harpactira* species) be kept under the best conditions. These include even temperatures of 27–30 °C throughout the day and night with humidity between 40 and 60%. Fresh water must also always be available.

Ceratogyrus species are excellent feeders and should be given one or two crickets almost daily. A vivarium for *Ceratogyrus* should contain a 10 cm deep layer of almost dry peat moss, a piece of tree bark or a halved flower pot as a hiding place and a water container. Pieces of earthenware pipes of different diameters are also useful as hiding places. The remainder of the "furnishings" will be provided by the spiders themselves, in that they will exca-

Fig. 105. *Ceratogyrus darlingi.*

vate a complicated system of burrows in which to live. This is quite a spectacle to watch.

Breeding: *Ceratogyrus darlingi* is not an easy species to breed. The greatest problem is presented by the animals themselves during mating. Both sexes are very sensitive and the female can be very aggressive. At the slightest disturbance, even a slight vibration caused by a footstep, the female will suddenly bite; the male will immediately flee from the "danger zone." One should then also be very wary of the male. In these circumstances it will immediately bite if an attempt is made to catch it. Four to six weeks after mating *C. darlingi* will produce an eggsac, containing up to 250 eggs, inside its living quarters. In contrast to those of many other tarantula species, the eggsac is not spherical. Instead it is attached to the living quarters and hangs in a stationary position. This is the brood protection carried out by this species. At a constant temperature of 26 °C the young hatch in about 3 weeks. They are tiny and eat only the smallest food such as *Drosophila* and springtails. They do, however, grow very quickly and the males can reach sexual maturity within a year.

Remarks: These aggressive and fast-moving spiders should only be handled by experienced enthusiasts. *Ceratogyrus darlingi* is one of the most interesting spiders from Africa. Keeping this species can give great pleasure. With good breeding stock,

regular reproduction should present no problems.

Citharischius crawshayi Pocock, 1900
King baboon tarantula

Distribution: Kenya
Maximum size: 9.5 cm
Description: A squat and very large African species. The powerful legs may be up to 7 mm in diameter. The rear legs are bent sharply inward, indicating that the species inhabits tunnels. The entire body is covered with short hairs. The abdomen does not have any urticating hairs. The entire animal is reddish-brown without any markings. With good feeding, its abdomen, like that of *Theraphosa blondi,* is almost spherical and may be 5 cm in diameter. The claws of the chelicerae also reach enormous dimensions; they may be up to 1.7 cm long.

Fig. 106. *Ceratogyrus darlingi,* male.

Fig. 107. *Citharischius crawshayi* in defensive posture.

Husbandry: A spacious vivarium at least 60 × 40 × 50 cm. A minimum 20–25 cm layer of relatively compact loam or soil should be used as substrate, the lower reaches of which should constantly be kept moist, while the surface is kept dry. A stack of flat rocks or a cork-bark tube should be installed to form an entrance to the burrow.

Below ground a constant temperature of 20–22 °C (using a heating cable) should be kept. On the surface it should be 22–25 °C during the day, falling to 20–22 °C at night. Depending upon the season, the humidity should be between 50 and 75%.

Occasionally they eat pink mice but otherwise large cockroaches, locusts and other large insects are its food. *Citharischius* is a powerful burrowing species. In its natural habitat in Kenya this spider is very rarely seen and can only be extracted from the laterite soil with great difficulty.

Nothing is known about its breeding habits. Recently, however, many egg-bearing females have been imported.

Behavior: This African species does not have any abdominal hairs which it can cast off for defensive purposes. If disturbed, it rears up on its hind legs. By rubbing the mouthparts together it produces a loud hissing and clicking noise. At the same time it opens the chelicerae wide and will not hesitate to bite. Once it has bitten, this species will not release its hold quickly.

Remarks: Anyone would be proud to have this species in a collection. No effort should be spared to breed these spiders. At present I am rearing around 200 spiderlings of this species from a female I brought home from Kenya.

Harpactira gigas Pocock, 1898
Baboon spider

Distribution: South Africa
Maximum size: 6 cm
Description: The *Harpactira* species are frequently confused with those of the

Fig. 108. *Citharischius crawshayi.*

genus *Pterinochilus,* but there is a significant difference in the shape of the bodies because the slenderly built *Pterinochilus* species remain relatively small.

Harpactira gigas is a very defensive species from Africa. If it is molested it will rear up, loudly stridulating, and strike at its aggressor with is pedipalps and forelegs. If the disturbance continues, this spider will not hesitate to inflict a severe bite. Furthermore, *H. gigas* may also suddenly leap from its vivarium. Once away from its accustomed surroundings it will run around wildly until it finds another hiding place.

Fig. 109. The very powerful hind legs of *C. crawshayi* are probably an adaptation to living in tunnels.

Fig. 110. *Harpactira gigas.*

As is the case with the American Avicularines the metatarsus and tarsus are equipped with powerful clinging pads. Although this spider can climb well they do not belong to the true arboreal species. The tibia and upper sides of the metatarsus and tarsus are covered in very long, light brown hairs. Newly molted animals appear to be pale pink in color. The abdomen is beige with black marbling. The black central line is partially interrupted. On both sides of this central line there are five black spots which become smaller streaks toward the rear. The carapace is black with a beige-colored cephalic part and radial stripes edged in beige. The underside of the femur has strong brush-like bunches of hairs. The sternum and underside of the femur are black. The underside of the abdomen is black with an orange-colored band in the region of the genitals and the book lungs. This spider is always prepared to bite, but its venom is totally harmless to humans and does not cause any pain.

Husbandry: Vivarium should be 20 × 30 × 20 cm. The substrate should be a mixture of peat moss and sand (1:1) around 7 cm deep. Prefabricated dwelling places in the form of cork-bark tubes will be readily accepted and further extended. These spiders do an enormous amount of spinning. Sometimes the entire vivarium may be completely "upholstered" with webs.

This species is very fond of heat. Localized temperatures up to 29 °C will frequently be sought out. There must, however, be cooler places in the vivarium. Average temperatures should be 25–28 °C during the day and 22–25 °C at night. Humidity should be 60–70%.

Remarks: *Harpactira* species are very susceptible to bacteria, mold and viral infections. Older and larger imported animals require a great deal of care and attention. After one or two molts, the greatest hurdles in getting the animal accustomed to a life in captivity have been overcome. After this *Harpactira* may even be kept by a beginner. The breeding of this species is usually hampered by a shortage of young or adult males, otherwise breeding should be quite easy.

The young are very susceptible to conditions which are too wet or too dry and are best reared in small containers having both moist and dry sections. *Harpactira gigas* is a very voracious feeder. The abdomen of an adult female may be the size of a chicken's egg.

Hysterocrates hercules Pocock, 1899
No common name

Distribution: Nigeria, West Africa
Maximum size: 8 cm
Description: A medium-sized, aggressive spider from West Africa and a very rare species. Its build is like that of *Citharischius crawshayi* but the legs are more slender. Also like *C. crawshayi* the rear legs are bent inward. This species lives in tunnels. The abdomen is oval and up to a diameter of 4 cm without urticating hairs. The legs are particularly hairy.

The ground color is a light beige or a short time after molting, a grayish-brown without any noteworthy pattern.

Husbandry: Vivarium at least 30 × 20 × 20 cm. Substrate semimoist peat or loamy earth at least 6 cm deep. Small cork tubes as entrances to the living "quarters" should be installed. Temperatures should be 20–25 °C during the day, 20 °C at night and localized in places up to 28 °C. Humidity should be around 70%. Lighting is not necessary. Because imminent molting is difficult to detect, it is vital that no uneaten food insects remain in the vivarium. It is a very easily kept species. In Germany this species has not yet been bred. The main reason is that to date no males have been imported. It would be wonderful if that were to happen soon. Anyone going to Nigeria on vacation should look out for these spiders.

The genus *Hysterocrates* is a group of very aggressive species. If molested they will rear up, spread the chelicerae and produce a loud stridulation noise. At the same time they drum their front legs on the ground. My single female once split a pen-

Fig. 111. *Hysterocrates hercules.*

cil which had been held against her. This species should only be approached with enormous respect.

Scodra griseipes Pocock, 1897
New taxonomy: *Stromatopelma griseipes* Pocock, 1897
No common name

Distribution: Ivory Coast
Maximum size: 5 cm
Description: Typical of the genus *Stromatopelma* are the very elongated forelegs with the large scopulae on the tarsus and metatarsus. The sides of the individual segments of the legs have very long hairs, especially on the tibia and metatarsus. These give the spider a very "hairy" appearance. The ground color of *S. griseipes* is beige to brown. The legs have a brown background with a row of black spots which are particularly easy to see on the tarsus and metatarsus.

It's a very fast-moving and aggressive species. Great care must be taken when handling this species because they will bite without warning.
Husbandry: The species *S. griseipes* lives on shrubs and bushes at about 80 cm above ground level. There it spins an enormous web. If the complete behavior pattern is to be seen, the vivarium must be suitably large. Dimensions of 30 × 30 × 40 cm are recommended.

Fig. 112. *Scodra griseipes* (new taxonomy: *Stromatopelma griseipes*).

Temperature during the day should be 22–29 °C, falling to 22 °C at night. Humidity should be around 60–70%. Pieces of bark should be glued to the internal walls of the vivarium and several climbing branches should be provided.
Remarks: *Stromatopelma griseipes* is only very rarely available and has not yet been bred in captivity because of a shortage of males. An experienced spider enthusiast will find this species relatively easy to keep.

Stromatopelma griseipes
(see *Scodra griseipes*)

Asiastic Species

Fig. 113. *Chilobrachys nitelinus.*

Chilobrachys nitelinus Karsch, 1891
Sri Lankan dwarf tarantula

Distribution: Sri Lanka, area around Knuckles
Maximum size: 2 cm
Description: A very small species of the subfamily Selenocosmiinae. It has an elongated carapace and when extremely satiated, a very long abdomen with relatively long spinnerets. This species has long slender legs with a ground color of light brown and a femur of black (in newly molted specimens) to brown.
Husbandry: Because *C. nitelinus* builds long horizontal tunnels on perpendicular slopes, it is almost impossible to keep them in a natural manner in the vivarium. *Chilobrachys nitelinus* is, however, extremely adaptable and may be comfortably housed in small plastic containers with a ground area of only 15 × 15 cm. In such a container *C. nitelinus* will soon construct a complicated system of tunnels. In its natural habitat, this species inhabits the same biotopes as the trapdoor spider in Fig. 24. Unfortunately, unlike the trapdoor spider, *C. nitelinus* does not occur in colonies and is only found individually. In Sri Lanka at the end of February 1988, I found only one specimen. For the arachnid enthusiast, this is an interesting species in comparison to other much larger tarantulas.

Haplopelma albostriatum
(see *Melopoeus albostriatum*)

Haplopelma lividum
(see *Lampropelma violaceopedes*)

Haplopelma minax
(see *Melopoeus minax*)

Lampropelma violaceopedes
Abraham, 1924
New taxonomy: *Haplopelma lividum*
Smith, 1990
Cobalt blue tarantula

Distribution: Burma, Singapore

Fig. 114. *Lampropelma violaceopedes* (new taxonomy: *Haplopelma lividum*).

Maximum size: 5 cm

Description: A small to medium-sized Asiatic species of the subfamily Ornithoctoninae. The carapace is gray and elongated with a very small, narrow thoracic groove. The abdomen is gray with a black central stripe and indistinct transverse banding. The entire spider is covered with only very short hair and is very slenderly built. It's a fast-moving and very aggressive spider and a typical tunnel dweller. Legs and pedipalps, with the exception of the tarsi, are vivid blue with a metallic sheen. It bites without any provocation.

Husbandry: This very beautiful species is not suitable for a beginner. They can not be kept in a normal vivarium for any length of time. They are best kept in a spacious, round container (such as a 5-liter pickling or preserve jar), two-thirds filled with a mixture of sand and peat. These spiders dig deep holes in the ground and may not leave these holes for several weeks. A check on their health is thus extremely difficult. Temperature should be around 23 °C. The substrate should be slightly moist but never wet. The drinking water container should be placed at the entrance to the dwelling tunnel. Although they initially feed well, many will quickly die. It could be that in the wild they only have a natural life expectancy of around 5 years.

Because of the large number of species and previous lack of interest in the subject, the systematics of Asiatic tarantulas has not yet been completely worked out. Many species are astoundingly similar in appearance. In this area of arachnology there is still a great deal of work to be done. One should, therefore, not be surprised when, in the current literature, several names are given for one and the same species. It would be wonderful if these misunderstandings could soon be cleared up by a fundamental reworking of the systematics of the Asiatic tarantula fauna.

Melopoeus albostriatum Simon, 1886
New taxonomy: *Haplopelma albostriatum* (Simon, 1886)
White striped tarantula

Distribution: Eastern Asia
Maximum size: 6 cm
Description: A slenderly built, tunnel-dwelling tarantula of the subfamily Ornithoctoninae. It's very frequently imported. The ground color is beige to brown and the patella, tibia and metatarsus each have two parallel white or cream stripes. The abdomen is a grayish brown with a black central stripe and transverse bands. This species is extremely aggressive.

Husbandry: Although *H. albostriatum* leads a subterranean existence, it adapts to life in the vivarium much better than other members of the subfamilies Selenocosmiinae and Ornithoctoninae.

The vivarium for this species should measure 20 × 30 × 20 cm and contain a

Fig. 115. *Melopoeus albostriatum* (new taxonomy: *Haplopelma albostriatum*).

layer of peat moss 7–10 cm deep. The substrate should be kept slightly moist and the temperature should never be above 25 °C. The roots of any plants installed in the vivarium will be damaged by the digging activities of the spider. A humidity of around 70% should be maintained. Pieces of bark will provide adequate refuges.

Among the spiders of Thailand, *H. albostriatum* is one of the "safer" species, since as a result of its markings it cannot be mistaken for any other species.

Haplopelma albostriatum is somewhat inactive, but this is compensated for by its attractive appearance, and it may be safely recommended to a novice. Breeding is,

Fig. 116. *Melopoeus minax,* male (new taxonomy: *Haplopelma minax*).

however, a matter of good fortune since systematic breeding is hindered by the fact that males are rarely imported. Newly imported females, however, usually lay eggs after only a short time in captivity. For tarantulas, the 100 eggs in each eggsac are nevertheless rather small.

Melopoeus minax Thorell, 1897
New taxonomy: *Haplopelma minax*
(Thorell, 1897)
Thailand black tarantula

Distribution: Sri Lanka, Borneo, Nias
Maximum size: 7 cm, usually smaller
Description: The most frequently imported Asian tarantula. With an imposing appearance it has thick, strong legs and the metatarsus and tarsus have large pads and a metallic iridescence. It also has an elongated carapace. Females are a deep black with brown-edged patella and tibia on the first pair of legs. The abdomen is dark gray with a black central stripe and black transverse stripes.

There is very prominent sexual dimorphism. Males which are not fully grown are similar to females in appearance. After the imaginal molt the legs of males are light brown from the patella to the metatarsus. The femur is black as is the tarsus, with a violet sheen. Pedipalps are also black. The carapace and abdomen are light brown with the black-striped pattern mentioned above. Very short, thick tibia spurs

grip the female's chelicerae during mating. Males are very slender and have long legs. Both sexes are extremely aggressive: at the slightest disturbance they will lunge out at the aggressor three or four times with the forelegs before biting. During this process the animals are in danger of their skin splitting at the joints. The fangs of adult females may be up to 13 mm long.

Husbandry: *Haplopelma* species are not suitable for a beginner. To be able to keep them for any length of time they must be provided with a deep substrate in which they will dig tunnels to live in. Regular checks and good hygiene are essential for successful husbandry. The secretive lifestyle of these animals makes it difficult to watch them carefully and they are often neglected. They drink frequently.

Haplopelma species are best kept in tall containers filled with earth which should not be allowed to dry out. A constant temperature of 25 °C is quite adequate. The species illustrated is an excellent feeder. It is very difficult to determine when skin molting is imminent; therefore, surplus food insects should not be left in the vivarium.

Breeding: This species has been bred frequently by experienced keepers. Mating is, however, usually only achieved with females that have been introduced to the male several days earlier. This is indicated by easily audible drumming noises. The number of eggs is amazingly small. My animals always laid between 37 and 70 eggs,

Fig. 117. *Melopoeus minax,* female (new taxonomy: *Haplopelma minax*).

each of which measured 5 mm. The young hatched after 6 to 8 weeks at 25 °C.

Poecilotheria bara
(see Poecilotheria subfusca)

Poecilotheria fasciata (Latreille, 1804)
Sri Lankan ornamental tarantula

Distribution: Sri Lanka
Maximum size: 7 cm

Description: An unmistakable, arboreal, climbing species of the subfamily Selenocosmiinae, group Poecilotherieae. The metatarsus and tarsus have very large adhesive pads. The upper sides of the femur, patella, tibia and metatarsus have yellow rings. On their undersides the limbs have lemon-yellow segments which give this creature a fascinating appearance. A very lively and fast-moving species, unfortunately it is somewhat aggressive.

Fig. 118. *Poecilotheria fasciata.*

Fig. 119. *Poecilotheria fasciata.*

Fig. 120. *Poecilotheria subfusca* (new taxonomy: *P. bara*).

Husbandry: A vivarium of 40 × 30 × 50 cm with several objects on which to climb. Like *P. cambridgei,* this species constructs large webs in its vivarium where it lives. Warm and bright areas are particularly sought out. The temperature should be between 25 and 27 °C with only a slight reduction at night. Humidity should be around 75%.

The main objective in keeping this magnificent species should be to attempt to get them to breed so that the offspring can be distributed among an even larger circle of arachnid enthusiasts.

Poecilotheria subfusca Pocock, 1895
New taxonomy: *Poecilotheria bara* Chamberlain, 1917

Distribution: Sri Lanka
Maximum size: 7–8 cm
Description: This species, which is slightly larger than *P. fasciata,* has almost

Fig. 121. (above left) Ventral surface of *P. fasciata*.

Fig. 122. (above right) Ventral surface of *P. subfusca* (new taxonomy: *P. bara*).

Fig. 123. (below) A molting young of *P. subfusca* (new taxonomy: *P. bara*) (after the second larval stage).

the same markings on its upper side. However, in comparison to *P. fasciata,* the femora of the two rear legs are completely black with a white ring at the end. This ring goes into the patella. This animal does, however, appear darker. In comparison to *P. fasciata* the underside of the femur is deep black.

Husbandry: Its management is similar to that of *P. fasciata.* Both species prefer dark refuges such as holes in branches. Bird nesting boxes may be used as a substitute. These correspond to the refuges found in their natural habitat in the tropical rain forest.

Breeding: This species has not yet been bred regularly in captivity. On 13 August 1988 a wild-caught female spun an eggsac. On 28 August 1988 the contents were placed in small petri dishes and transferred to an incubator at 25 °C and 100% humidity. The spiderlings hatched on 29 and 31 August 1988.

To accelerate the development of the young, the incubation temperature was increased to 26 °C. On 14 September their legs turned black. Three days later they molted for the first time. Around 70 young were reared and will hopefully form the nucleus of future breeding colonies in Germany.

Remarks: Look out for parasitic mites! These tend to congregate in inaccessible places and it is imperative that they are removed from their host animal (with a fine artist's brush). It has proven expedient to place the spider in a large jar containing ether fumes (highly flammable!). In this jar, most of the mites will fall from the spider.

Bibliography

Bellmann, H. (1984): Spinnen beobachten—bestimmen. Neumann—Neudamm, Melsungen.

Bristowe, W. S. (1971): The World of Spiders. Collins New Naturalist, London.

Bücher, W. (1952): Instintos maternais nas aranhas brasileiras. Dusenia II (6): 57.

———— (1956): Südamerikanische Spinnen und ihre Gifte. Arzneimittel-Forschung (6): 293.

———— (1971): Spiders. In: Venomous Animals and their Venoms. Academic Press, New York/London.

———— Das Haus der Gifte.

Comstock, J. (1940): The Spider Book. Comstock Press, Ithaca.

Cooke, J. et al. (1972): The urticating hairs of Theraphosid Spiders. American Museum Novitates 2498: 1–43.

Foelix, R. F.: Biologie der Spinnen. Georg Thieme Verlag, Stuttgart.

Friederich, U., and Volland, W. (1981): Futtertierzucht. Eugen Ulmer Verlag, Stuttgart.

Gertsch, W. (1949): American Spiders. Van Nostrand & Co., New York.

Harms, K. H.: Rote Liste der Spinnen (Araneae). In BLAB, J., et al. (Hrsg.): Rote Liste der gefährdeten Tiere und Pflanzen in der BRD. Kilda-Verlag, Greven.

Hubert, M. (1979): Les Araignees, Boubeé, Paris.

Jones, D. (1983): The Country Life Guide to Spiders of Britain and Northern Europe. Hamlyn Publishing Group, Feltham.

Kaston, B. (1978): How to Know the Spiders. W. C. Brown Co., Dubuque, Iowa.

Klaas, P. (1988): Haarige Gesellen. Aquarien und Terrarien-Magazin 2.

Kullmann, E., and Stern, H. (1975): Leben am seidenen Faden. Bertelsmann Verlag, München.

Levi, H., and L. (1968): A Guide to Spiders and their Kin. Golden Press, New York.

McCook, H. (1869, 1890 & 1893): American Spiders and their Spinning Work. I–III., Philadelphia.

McCrone, J., and Levi, H. (1964): North American Widow Spiders. Psyche 71, 1:12–27.

Melchers, M. (1964): Zur Biologie der Vogelspinnen. Z. Morph. Ökol. Tiere 53: 517.

Schmidt, G. (1986): Spinnen. Lehrmeister-Bücherei. A.-Philler-Verlag, Minden.

Schmidt, G. (1952): Spinnenpflege in Terrarien. DATZ 12: 89.

———— (1958): Vogelspinnen und ihre Gifte. Orion 13: 545.

———— (1959): Vogelspinnen im Terrarium. DATZ 12: 89.

———— (1986): Vogelspinnen. Lebensweise. Bestimmungsschlüssel. Haltung. Zucht. A. Philler-Verlag, Minden.

Weygoldt, P. (1966): Moos- und Bücher-
    skorpione. Neue Brehm-Bücherei.
    Ziemsen-Verlag, W. Henberg.

Wiehle, H. (1954): Aus den Spinnenleben
    wärmerer Länder. A. Ziemsen Verlag,
    Wittenberg Lutherstadt.

Photographic Sources

	Figure no.
Matthias Forst, Cologne	4, 6, 7, 11, 15, 16, 67, 68, 69, 74, 75, 80
Klaus Wassman, Munich	1, 19
Kurt Nicholaisen, Arhus	2, 23
Rainer Stawikowski, Essen	3, 3a, 17, 18
Holger Ehmke, Kiel	45

All other photographs by the author.

Drawings by Klaus Richter, Düsseldorf.

Index